WADSWORTH PHILOSOPHERS SERIES

ON
POPPER

Mark Amadeus Notturno
University of Virginia

THOMSON

™

WADSWORTH

Australia • Canada • Mexico • Singapore • Spain • United Kingdom • United States

For more information about our
products, contact us at:
**Thomson Learning Academic
Resource Center
1-800-423-0563**

For permission to use material from
this text, contact us by:
Phone: 1-800-730-2214
Fax: 1-800-731-2215
Web: www.thomsonrights.com

Asia
Thomson Learning
5 Shenton Way #01-01
UIC Building
Singapore 068808

Australia
Nelson Thomson Learning
102 Dodds Street
South Street
South Melbourne, Victoria 3205
Australia

Canada
Nelson Thomson Learning
1120 Birchmount Road
Toronto, Ontario M1K 5G4
Canada

Europe/Middle East/South Africa
Thomson Learning
High Holborn House
50-51 Bedford Row
London WC1R 4LR
United Kingdom

Latin America
Thomson Learning
Seneca, 53
Colonia Polanco
11560 Mexico D.F.
Mexico

Spain
Paraninfo Thomson Learning
Calle/Magallanes, 25
28015 Madrid, Spain

For Werner and Annette Baumgartner

Contents

Preface

Karl Popper (1902-1994) is recognized around the world as one of the twentieth century's greatest philosophers of science and as one of its most articulate and influential critics of Marxism and closed society. Popper was an outspoken champion of rationalism, and a constant critic of subjectivist and authoritarian tendencies in science and society. He is famous for his falsifiability criterion of demarcation between science and metaphysics, but is more important for his fallibilism, for his identification of rationality with the critical attitude, for his critique of induction, and for his characterization of science as a never-ending problem-solving activity that grows through trial and error. He is, perhaps, most important for his defense of open society and the freedom of thought. Popper was a critic of determinist theories of science and society, and a proponent of free will. And he was, in his later years, a proponent of evolutionary epistemology, of a dualism between body and mind, and of the idea that our theories, problems, and artifacts in general belong to an objective but immaterial 'World 3'.

Popper used to tell his students that there is no such thing as a scientific method other than the method of trial and error. This simple idea has initiated a revolutionary way of thinking in philosophy and science. Popper thought that we are all in search of a better world. And he taught that, instead of uncritically accepting our theories and beliefs on authority or trying to justify them with appeals to reason and experience, we should search for problems and inconsistencies in them and try to eliminate them as best we can. Instead of trying to prove that we are right, we should try to find the ways in which we are wrong. He summed up his entire philosophy with the words:

'I may be wrong and you may be right,
and by an effort, we may get nearer to the truth.'

Mark Notturno
Washington, DC
October, 2001

Acknowledgements

I want to thank Dan Kolak for inviting me to write this book on Popper. I also want to thank the people who helped me. Werner and Annette Baumgartner, Robert Hobart, Jim Baer, and the Board of Directors of the Ianus Foundation provided the necessary financial and moral support. Werner Baumgartner, Stefano Gattei, David Horrobin, Paul Humphreys, and Allan Megill read chapters of the book and made helpful comments. Bob Dylan and Clifford Brown helped a lot. And the spirit of Karl Popper was always at my side.

My son Karl, who is now old enough to be proud that he is named after Popper, allowed me to spend time writing when I really should have been playing with him. And Kira Viktorova—who is my wife, colleague, critic, and best friend—is also the best possible muse that a writer can have.

1

The Logic of Scientific Discovery

Karl Popper's great work in the philosophy of science is *The Logic of Scientific Discovery*, a book that was first published in German as *Logik der Forschung* in 1934, and translated into English only in 1959. A.J. Ayer called the book 'a work of great originality and power'. It introduces Popper's critique of induction as scientific method and his 'falsifiability criterion of demarcation', which together constitute his philosophy of science. Its title, however, may seem a bit misleading. Philosophers and scientists have for centuries dreamt of a 'logic of discovery', by which they meant a mechanical method, or algorithm, for discovering new theories and showing that they are true. Popper, however, denied that anything like a 'logic of discovery' in this sense exists. So anyone who approaches his book with the expectation of finding one will probably be disappointed. This disappointment may, to some extent, be due to bad translation. It is true that the German term '*Forschung*' is still sometimes used in the sense of the English term 'discovery'. But it is more often used in the sense of 'research', and 'the logic of scientific research' would, in many ways, have been a more accurate title for the book. There is, however, a sense in which 'the logic of scientific discovery' is an apt description of Popper's idea of scientific method, even though it is not what most readers might expect. And there is, moreover, good reason to think that Popper chose the title with this in mind. For in one of the epigrams to the book, he cites Lord Acton as saying:

There is nothing more necessary to the man of science than its history, and the logic of discovery...: the way error is detected, the use of hypothesis, of imagination, the mode of testing.[1]

And this, I suggest, is the way that Popper understood the term.

Popper used to tell his students that he proposed falsifiability as the logic of scientific discovery in an effort to replace Science with a capital 'S' with science with a small 's': that he wanted, in other words, to show that science is a human affair, and a highly fallible affair; that scientists make mistakes just like everyone else, and perhaps even more than other people because they have more opportunities to make them; that the best we can do in science is to try to eliminate our errors; and, most important, that there is no such thing as a Scientific Knowledge that can speak *ex cathedra*. There are still many people who believe that science can and should speak *ex cathedra*. But if we understand 'the logic of scientific discovery' in Acton's sense, then the title may begin to make more than a little sense.

In the Preface I mentioned Popper's fallibilism. This idea—that human beings and their scientific knowledge are inherently fallible and subject to error—was still controversial in the 1930's when Popper published his *Logik der Forschung*. But the idea is now accepted by most contemporary philosophers of science, and it is *not* the most distinctive feature of Popper's epistemology. The most distinctive feature of Popper's epistemology, and the key to understanding his general philosophical outlook, is his rejection of the idea that scientific knowledge is justified true belief. Popper thought that this idea, which I will here call '*justificationism*', has led many philosophers of science to focus upon epistemological problems that are irrelevant to scientific knowledge. His own '*anti-justificationism*' is closely related to fallibilism. But it is also somewhat different. For while most Western philosophers now acknowledge that even the very best of our scientific knowledge is fallible, they continue to regard it as rational and objective only to the extent to which it is justified. 'We cannot', they acknowledge, 'justify our scientific theories by showing that they are actually true. But we may be able to justify them by showing that they are probably true. And we can, at the very least, show that our own belief in them is justified'. Popper, however, denies that we can show that our theories are true, or even probably true. And while he thought that we may be able to justify our preference for one theory as opposed to another, he also thought that whether or not our *beliefs* are justified is completely beside the point when it comes to science. Where most

2

philosophers of science are concerned with the problem of showing that and why our theories are justified, or at least that and why we are justified in believing them, Popper was concerned with explaining how we can subject our theories to empirical tests, and how we can get rid of those theories that do not survive critical scrutiny.

The idea that scientific knowledge is and must be justified has a very long tradition in the history of Western philosophy. Indeed, most Western philosophers believe that knowledge is a kind of justified true belief, and that its justification is what makes it objective and rational, and what distinguishes it from subjective faith. Philosophical questions regarding the objectivity and rationality of a theory are thus typically questions regarding its justification, where the justification itself is construed as a logical argument that has the theory to be justified as its conclusion and statements reporting the evidence that is supposed to justify it as its premises. To show that such an argument is invalid, or that it relies upon false or even questionable premises, is to undercut that theory's claim to be justified true belief—and, thus, its claim to be objective and rational knowledge. Fallibilists who regard knowledge in this way—and this, again, includes most philosophers in the Western tradition—typically regard *scientific* knowledge as a kind of knowledge whose justification is much greater than the justification that we have for the ordinary knowledge claims that we make in life. This greater justification, they say, is what justifies the greater authority that we rightfully attribute to it.

But the idea that scientific knowledge cannot be justified also has a very long tradition in the history of Western philosophy. It is, in fact, the tradition of Western skepticism, which often seems definitive of the history of philosophy itself. Indeed, Western philosophy, at least since Descartes, has often appeared to be a contest between the cognitivist and the skeptic. The cognitivist in this game claims to know that a certain statement, proposition, theory, or fact is true. His task is to present arguments to show that and why his claim is justified. The skeptic, on the other hand, claims to doubt that the statement that the cognitivist claims to know is true—or, at the very least, that it is or can be justified. His task is to present arguments to show why the cognitivist's alleged justification does not really work. Skepticism, as it pertains to science, is the denial that any scientific theory can be justified or shown to be true, or that it has any special claim to authority. This is precisely the position that Popper maintains. Yet Popper insists that we do have scientific knowledge and he is adamantly opposed to skepticism. *Scientific* knowledge, according to Popper, cannot and need not be justified at all. Fallibilists who maintain that our scientific knowledge is and must be justified typically feel that serious people simply do not claim to know something without any good reason at all. Popper certainly shared that attitude, but he thought that this was not a good reason to think that scientific knowledge can or must be justified.

The claim that scientific research is both rational and objective but that its theories are neither justified, necessarily true, nor even necessarily believed thus goes well beyond what most fallibilists say. It proposes a radical change in our very concept of knowledge, which can be seen by the fact that most fallibilists still regard the idea of unjustified rational knowledge as a contradiction in terms. It also marks a radical shift in many of the traditional problems of knowledge. Philosophers who say that scientific knowledge cannot be justified are usually regarded as skeptics, and anyone who regards knowledge as justified true belief will probably regard Popper as a skeptic as well. But there is a big difference between Popper's position and the skeptic's. They both maintain that we cannot justify our knowledge. But the skeptic says that scientific knowledge must be justified in order to be rational and objective, and Popper explains how scientific knowledge can be objective and rational despite the fact that it cannot be justified. The skeptic demands justification, and bemoans the fact that we cannot achieve it. Popper, on the contrary, says that scientific knowledge need not be justified, but that we must be able to test it against reason and experience instead.

This, however, changes everything.

For if Popper is right that we *do* have scientific knowledge, that it *cannot* be justified, but that it is, nonetheless, both *objective* and *rational*, then it follows that:

1.   Scientific knowledge can no longer be regarded as justified true belief, *since no statement can be justified;*
2.   The rationality of scientific knowledge can no longer be regarded as a product of its justification, *since no statement can be justified;*
3.   The objectivity of scientific knowledge can no longer be regarded as a product of its justification, *since no statement can be justified;*
4.   Skepticism—or the denial that we have knowledge—can no longer be regarded as the thesis that no statement can be justified, *since no statement can be justified;*
5.   Justifying theories can no longer be regarded as a task for philosophy and science, *since no statement can be justified;*
6.   Logical arguments can no longer be regarded as attempts to justify statements, *since no statement can be justified*; and

7. The criticism that a statement or theory is not justified can no longer be regarded as a criticism, *since no statement can be justified.*

So it is important, before going any further, to understand how Popper was led to this shift. In this chapter I will suggest that this can best be understood as his response to the collapse of traditional 'bedrock' foundationalism.

Foundationalism

Traditional 'bedrock' foundationalism said that knowledge must be justified in order to be rational, and it attempted to justify our knowledge by deriving it from an indubitable and infallible source. René Descartes initiated the foundationalist program by saying that we must first doubt whatever we can doubt if we are ever to be certain of anything at all. It is only in this way, he said, that we could arrive at a certain and indubitable foundation. Descartes did not propose to doubt his beliefs one by one. He instead asked whether the sources from which he derived them were reliable. He recognized sense perception and pure reason as two possible sources of knowledge. But he argued that sense perception is too fallible to serve as a source of certain knowledge, and that we know objects through *a priori* reason instead. Descartes said that his God-given intellect was an infallible source of knowledge, and that whatever he clearly and distinctly perceived with it must be true. He thus attempted to 'ground' scientific knowledge on his 'proofs' that God exists and is not a deceiver. But many philosophers found his 'rationalism' unconvincing, and by the eighteenth century the so-called 'empiricists' had grown skeptical of *a priori* reason and of the attempt to ground scientific knowledge upon it. Empiricism regarded sense experience as the only criterion of truth. It said that our scientific theories must be justified 'inductively' by observation and sense experience, and that beliefs that cannot be justified in this way should be 'committed to the flames'. The empiricists agreed with Descartes that we should begin by purging our minds of all theories or, as Francis Bacon called them, 'anticipations of the mind'. But they said that we should then proceed by making careful and repeated observations, from which we could infer universal theories. Inductive inference, according to this model, serves as a method both for discovering new theories and for justifying them. We discover general theories by inferring them from sense observations. And if we collect our observations in the right way, and if our inductive inferences are 'correct', then the observations will also serve as their justification.

5

This account of scientific discovery and justification seemed like a plausible model of how theory is related to observation. But David Hume then pointed out that all inductive arguments are invalid. Hume said that there is no 'middle term' in an inductive inference that allows us to validly infer future events from past experiences. No matter how many times we have seen the sun rise in the past, it is always possible that it will not rise again tomorrow. No matter how many observations we might make, the corresponding universal theory that generalizes them might always be false. Hume's critique of induction is a problem for any attempt to rationally justify or confirm the universal theories of science by observation and experience. The invalidity of inductive inference means that observation can provide only *psychological*, as opposed to *rational*, justification through custom and habit. Hume, however, argued that we have no choice but to reason inductively from experience. Induction, he said, is logically invalid but psychologically necessary. And he concluded that reason is and ought to be the slave of the passions.

It was this idea, Immanuel Kant tells us, that awoke him from his 'dogmatic slumbers'. Kant realized that Hume's empiricism leads to irrationalism by saying that scientific knowledge is based not upon reason, but upon custom and habit. Kant rejected irrationalism, and—thinking that Hume was right to think that empiricism entailed it—concluded that we must have *a priori* knowledge after all. Kant pointed to Euclid's geometry and Newton's physics as examples of '*a priori* synthetic' knowledge. He said that these sciences consist of strictly universal, necessary, and certain truths that cannot be based upon sense experience alone. They are not, he argued, analytic truths—or statements that can be known to be true through an analysis of their meaning—but they are strictly universal, necessary, and certain nonetheless. Kant never doubted the *a priori* synthetic character of these sciences. He instead tried to explain how a science can be *a priori* synthetic by talking about a 'Copernican Revolution' in epistemology. Nature, he said, does not impress its laws upon our minds, as Hume thought. Our minds, on the contrary, impose their laws upon nature in order to understand it—and this imposition is rational and objective because all rational minds impose the same laws. But Kant's attempt to account for the objectivity and rationality of science collapsed when Einstein imposed a non-Newtonian physics and a non-Euclidean geometry upon nature. Einstein described a natural world that rational beings before him had never conceived. And his descriptions were corroborated by the predictions that he derived from his theories in order to test them.

1. The Logic of Scientific Discovery

Einstein shattered all hopes of explaining the rationality of science in terms of *a priori* foundations. If Kant could be wrong about the *a priori* certainty of Newton's physics and Euclid's geometry, then how could anyone claim to be *a priori* certain again? But it did not quite shatter the hopes of foundationalists, who, forgetting about Hume, once again tried to explain the rationality of science as a byproduct of its justification by sense experience. Ludwig Wittgenstein and the logical positivists, who were Popper's contemporaries in Vienna, argued that empirical verifiability is what distinguishes science from metaphysics, and sense from nonsense. They said that science must eschew *a priori* synthetic statements, and that a statement is meaningful if-and-only-if it is analytically true or empirically verifiable. This was their famous 'verifiability criterion of meaning'. It maintains that science is not only rational knowledge, but the only form of discourse that can even be regarded as meaningful. This was undoubtedly the most influential foundationalist program of the twentieth century. But it is important to understand that Wittgenstein and the positivists, like Descartes, Hume, and Kant before them, regarded knowledge as justified true belief. They all said that scientific knowledge is objective and rational to the extent to which it is justified, and that an argument is a justification of knowledge to the extent to which it is rational and objective.

Indeed, the whole point of a foundationalist program is to give an objective and rational justification that is as compelling for others as it is for ourselves.

This idea of objective and rational justification gave rise to many foundationalist projects in the history of Western philosophy, each of which claimed to give objective and rational justifications that would be compelling for all rational beings. But the fact that there have been so many foundationalist projects in the history of Western philosophy is due to the fact that foundationalists, ironically enough, could never quite agree about what is or ought to be regarded as objective, rational, and compelling. They all conceived of science as a building that must be grounded, through the cement of logic, upon a firm foundation. They all hoped, in this way, to build story after story upon their foundations so as to produce a skyscraper of science in which the social sciences in the penthouse would be just as objective, and rational, and certain as the natural and mathematical sciences in the basement. And they did not, insofar as this is concerned, differ too much in proclaiming that their favorite 'objective and rational foundations' are 'indubitable', and 'self-evident', and 'clear and distinct', and 'infallibly true', etc., etc.

7

ECONOMICS
SOCIOLOGY
PSYCHOLOGY
BIOLOGY
CHEMISTRY
PHYSICS
MATHEMATICS
LOGIC
THE INDUBITABLE, SELF-EVIDENT, CLEAR AND DISTINCT, INFALLIBLE ETC., ETC., OBJECTIVE AND RATIONAL FOUNDATIONS

But it should be clear that there is something fundamentally wrong with the foundationalist picture, if only because the so-called 'objective and rational' infallible foundations are typically characterized in terms of subjective, indeed *psychological*, predicates.

Popper held that the convictions of a person or a group of people can never justify the claim that a statement is true. Our psychological experiences may lead us to regard a statement as clear and distinct, self-evident, and indubitable. But such experiences are too subjective to show that a statement is true, let alone infallible. These ideas play a major role in his solution to the problems of induction and demarcation. But this solution, which I will discuss in the next chapter, stems from his anti-justificationism.

Popper's Problem

Popper thought that the attempt to explain the objectivity and rationality of science as byproducts of its justification had failed. We cannot justify our scientific theories with *a priori* reason because *a priori* reason is fallible, and we cannot justify them with sense experience because sense experience is fallible as well. He argued that the foundationalist's demand that we justify our knowledge by rational argument inevitably leads to subjectivism and irrationalism in the foundations themselves—so if we want to avoid Hume's conclusion that scientific knowledge is *irrationally* grounded in custom and habit, then we have to explain how it can be rational *given* the fact that it cannot be rationally justified. This was Popper's problem. In order to solve it, he had to offer an alternative to the foundationalists' view that the objectivity and rationality of scientific knowledge depends upon its justification. He had to explain how science can be objective and rational despite the fact that it cannot show that its theories are true.

Here, Popper agreed with Hume that the attempt to justify our knowledge inductively from experience leads to irrationalism—but he denied that scientists generally reason in this way at all. He agreed with Kant that experience and observation presuppose *a priori* ideas—but he denied that our *a priori* ideas are certainly true. And he agreed with Wittgenstein and the positivists that it is no longer possible to appeal to *a priori* synthetic principles in our attempts to justify natural science— but he argued that metaphysical theories need not be meaningless, and that verifiability, in any event, cannot be the demarcation between science and metaphysics, because it fails to account for the scientific character of scientific laws, which cannot be verified through inductive arguments from experience.

But while Descartes, Hume, Kant, Wittgenstein, and the positivists agreed that scientific knowledge must be justified in order to be objective and rational, Popper cut the Gordian knot by arguing that scientific knowledge cannot, and need not, be justified at all—and by saying that it is objective and rational not because we have justified it, but because we can test it. Popper argued in *The Logic of Scientific Discovery* that the demand that we justify our knowledge by objective and rational argument leads to a trilemma. For it leads either to *infinite regress*—in which the demand that we justify a statement is replaced by the demand that we justify the statements that justify it—or to attempts to cut short the infinite regress by 'grounding' our knowledge upon the authority of reason or the authority of experience. In the one case, the demand for justification leads to *dogmatism*. In the other, it leads to *psychologism*.

JUSTIFICATION

DOGMATISM	*PSYCHOLOGISM*
(Classical Rationalism)	(Classical Empiricism)

INFINITE REGRESS

In either case, it leads to a *reductio ad absurdum* of the idea that we can justify our knowledge with objective and rational argument. For in order to avoid the infinite regress, we must ultimately accept the truth of some statement (or the reliability of some cognitive source) without justification. We can always say that the truth of this statement (or the reliability of this source) is clear and distinct, self-evident, indubitable, etc., etc. But this only underscores the fact that it is not really justified. And the fact that we accept it without justification means that we attribute an authority to it that we deny to others. Thus, where Wittgenstein and the positivists demanded that our knowledge be justified by experience, Popper argued that 'the main problem of philosophy is the critical analysis of the appeal to the authority of 'experience'— precisely that 'experience' which every latest discoverer of positivism is, as ever, artlessly taking for granted'.[2]

But if the objectivity and rationality of our knowledge is based upon its justification, and its justification is ultimately based upon authority, then it is difficult to see why our knowledge is not ultimately subjective and irrational after all.

Most twentieth century philosophers faced with this trilemma have opted either for psychologism or for some form of dogmatism. They have, by so doing, weakened either their concept of justification, since neither dogmatism nor psychologism can show that a statement is true; or their concept of truth, by defining it in terms of what is either psychologistically or dogmatically justified; or very frequently both. Inductivists, insofar as this is concerned, have *doubly* weakened their idea of justification—first by appealing to *psychologism* to justify the singular observation statements that serve as premises in inductive arguments, and then by appealing to *dogmatism* by using invalid argument forms, in which the conclusion can be false even if all of the premises are true, to justify the universal theories that they 'derive' as their conclusions.

Popper, when faced with these alternatives, is nearly alone in maintaining the traditional philosophical concepts of justification and truth—according to which the justification of a theory would show that it is true, and 'true' means 'corresponding to the facts'—and giving up the idea that justification is a necessary condition for knowledge. But this, as I have said, changes everything. For quite aside from anything else, it changes the entire problem situation in epistemology and the philosophy of science.

Many philosophers today tell us that they have given up Descartes' project of 'bedrock' foundationalism. But they have often replaced it with a justificationist program that would 'ground' our knowledge upon a subjective 'commitment' to a belief, or theory, or paradigm that they regard as neither justified nor rational. We can see this approach in the later philosophies of Wittgenstein, Carnap, and Quine; in Thomas Kuhn's theory of scientific paradigms, and in Richard Rorty's appeal to 'solidarity' as a substitute for objectivity. These philosophers tell us that scientific knowledge can indeed be justified. But they also say that its justification is always tentative, fallible, and precarious—and, in any event, ultimately based upon commitment—forgetting, perhaps, the reason why we wanted a justification in the first place. I like to call their approach 'floating foundationalism', since it retains the foundationalist theory of rationality and its demand for justification by logical argument, but leaves the foundations themselves floating in midair. But the problem of knowledge, if Popper is right, can no longer be the problem of justifying our theories—for no foundation is grounded upon bedrock, and those that float in midair cannot show that our theories are true or even probably true.

So what is objective and rational scientific knowledge, for Popper, if not justified true belief?

An answer to this question will begin to emerge in the next chapter as we work our way through the solutions that Popper proposed to the problems of demarcation and induction. But a more complete answer will have to await our discussion of 'World 3'—the world of the objective products of the human mind, including scientific problems and theories. For now, suffice it to say, once again, that Popper conceived of the logic of scientific discovery not as the logic of discovering and justifying our theories, but as the logic of discovering our errors.

Endnotes

[1] Karl R. Popper, *The Logic of Scientific Discovery*, Hutchinson, London, 1959. Reprinted by Routledge, London and New York, 1992, p. 14.

[2] Popper, *The Logic of Scientific Discovery*, pp. 51-2.

2
Conjectures and Refutations

Popper's idea of objective and rational—albeit unjustified—scientific knowledge is closely related to his idea that a scientific theory should be *falsifiable*. This idea is easily misunderstood. And in this chapter I will try to explain what it means.

Popper believed that our scientific knowledge is fallible; that it grows through conjecture and refutation, which is just another way of saying that it grows through trial and error; and that the claim that a theory is justified is an appeal to authority that unwittingly leads to subjectivism, irrationalism, and skepticism when we learn that it is not. He equated the rational attitude with the critical attitude, and he called his philosophy 'critical rationalism' in order to emphasize the role of testing in science. He said that objective scientific knowledge consists not of justified true beliefs, but of speculative conjectures, guesses, or hypotheses that we put forth in our attempt to solve scientific problems. We are rational as scientists to the extent to which we are willing to test our guesses with logical arguments. And our guesses themselves are *scientific,* in the empirical sense, to the extent to which they may conflict with the empirical observation reports that we use as premises in these arguments. The invalidity of inductive inference means that our tests can never show that a theory is true, or even probably true—for our observations may always be better explained by theories that we have yet to conceive. But we can, by using deductive logic, sometimes infer from our observation reports that an empirical theory is false. Science aims at truth, or at least at getting closer to the truth. But it progresses by testing our theories, and not by showing that they are true. Empirical observations, for this reason, are better understood as attempts to refute our theories, and not as attempts to justify them.

This, as a first approximation, is what Popper meant when he said that a scientific theory should be 'falsifiable'. In what follows, I will try to put some flesh on this skeleton by explaining how falsifiability is an attempt to solve the problems of induction and demarcation.

Induction and Demarcation

Popper regarded induction and demarcation as the 'two fundamental problems of epistemology'.[1] The first of these, which he traced to Hume, asks whether or to what extent empirical observation and experiment can rationally justify a strictly universal theory. The second, which he traced to Kant, asks how we can distinguish real scientific theories from metaphysical and 'pseudo-scientific' theories. Popper tells us that he first discovered the problem of demarcation, and only several years later came to appreciate its relationship to the problem of induction. But it is easy enough to see the connection. For classical empiricism maintains that scientific theories are distinguished from metaphysical and 'pseudo-scientific' theories by their being the product of a proper application of the inductive method. This view was empiricist dogma in the 1930's when Popper wrote his *Logik der Forschung*, and it is still prevalent even today. It says that real scientific theories are both discovered and justified by inductive generalization from empirical observations. So it is, perhaps, best to explain Popper's solution to the problem of demarcation, as Popper himself sometimes did, by first explaining his solution to the problem of induction.

Hume's Problem

In chapter 1 I said that Hume pointed out that there is no 'middle term' in arguments that infer future events from past experiences, and that arguments from singular statements to strictly universal statements are *invalid*. Now it is often thought that the problem of induction is a problem of uncertainty—that since inductive inferences are invalid, we can never be certain of their conclusions. But this is not the way that Hume and Popper understood the problem. If the problem of induction were a problem about uncertainty, then there would be a problem of deduction as well. For a valid deductive argument cannot insure that its conclusion is true—let alone certainly true. Its validity means only that its conclusion must be true *if its premises are true*. But this means that (one or more of) its premises must be false if its conclusion is. Valid arguments may have true premises and true conclusions. But they may also have false premises. And if they do, then their conclusions may be either true or false.

Indeed, the only thing that the validity of an argument tells us regarding the truth of its premises and conclusion is that it cannot be the case that the premises are true and the conclusion false.

It is important to understand this point. Hume is often regarded as a skeptic who believed that scientific theories cannot be certain. This, however, misses the point of his argument. Hume believed that we *can* be certain that scientific theories are true, despite the fact that inductive arguments are invalid. But he argued that our certainty is not based upon reason, but upon custom and habit instead. He said that the conclusions of inductive arguments do not rationally follow from their premises, yet we are psychologically compelled to believe them nonetheless. This, in a nutshell, is what Popper meant when he said that Hume's epistemology leads to irrationalism.

Popper agreed with Hume that inductive inferences are invalid. But he regarded the idea of inductive method as a myth. Scientists typically do not derive their theories inductively from observations. They invent them instead as speculative solutions to scientific problems. He thought that observation may sometimes play a role in suggesting a theory to a scientist. But he argued that it frequently does not—and that it rarely, if ever, plays quite the role that the inductive method suggests. For scientists generally do not purge their minds of all prior theories, and they generally do not infer their theories from careful and repeated observations. Indeed, Popper argued that we *cannot* both purge our minds of all prior theories *and* make careful observations. 'If I tell you to "Observe!"' he said, 'then you will most probably ask "Observe what?"' His point was partly that observation is driven by theory. But it was also that the whole inductivist idea about the relationship between theory and observation is wrong. We do not and cannot infer universal theories from observations, for real scientific theories are simply too abstract for that. We instead propose scientific theories as speculative solutions to scientific problems, and we then try to deduce observable consequences from them. These deductions are sometimes made in an attempt to explain the 'facts' that we have already observed, and sometimes in an attempt to predict or retrodict 'facts' that we have not. But in each case, our predictions and retrodictions follow as valid deductive consequences of our theory—taken, of course, in conjunction with initial conditions and auxiliary hypotheses. They can thus serve as one-sided tests of these premises. Their falsity shows that something is wrong in the conjunction of theory, initial conditions, and auxiliary hypotheses. But their truth shows only that the premises have thus far survived the test.

Hume rejected induction as rational inference, but he accepted it as both our psychology of learning and the method of empirical science. Popper, on the other hand, rejected induction as bad psychology, because it ignores the fact that we have inborn expectations—such as the expectations that we will find food, light, and oxygen in our environment—that are actually built into our bodily organs. He also rejected it as bad methodology, partly because it says that scientists should do what they cannot do, and partly because he saw it as a way to claim authority for theories that are not really justified. Inductivism says that sense experience justifies our theories as habitual expectations. It thus subordinates reason to custom and habit, or consensus and solidarity, and says that reason is and ought to be the slave of the passions. But Popper said that science appeals to experience to *test* its theories—not to *justify* them—and that the test subordinates consensus and habit to reason. This is where his idea that scientific theories are distinguished by their falsifiability comes in.

Kant's Problem

Popper tells us that he began to grapple with the problem of demarcation in 1919. This was the year that he began to have doubts about communism and psychoanalysis, and the year that he first heard Einstein speak. He says that:

> The problem which troubled me at the time was neither, 'When is a theory true?' nor, 'When is a theory acceptable?' My problem was different. *I wished to distinguish between science and pseudoscience*; knowing very well that science often errs, and that pseudoscience may happen to stumble on the truth.[2]

Popper was greatly impressed by Einstein, and especially by the difference between his critical attitude and the attitude of the Marxists and Freudians in Vienna. Marx, Freud, and Einstein each claimed that their theories were scientific. But Marxists and Freudians claimed that their theories were equally confirmed by contradictory events, and Einstein explained how his theory might actually be tested and shown to be false. Popper began to think that a theory that can explain anything that can possibly happen doesn't really explain anything at all. He also began to have doubts about psychoanalysis' claim that its theories were verified by 'clinical observations'. A conversation that he had with the psychologist Alfred Adler, for whom he worked as a volunteer, made a strong impression:

I reported to him a case which to me did not seem particularly Adlerian, but which he found no difficulty in analysing in terms of his theory of inferiority feelings, although he had not even seen the child. Slightly shocked, I asked him how he could be so sure. 'Because of my thousandfold experience', he replied; whereupon I could not help saying: 'And with this new case, I suppose, your experience has become thousand-and-one-fold.'[3]

Popper drew the following conclusions:

(1) It is easy to obtain confirmations, or verifications, for nearly every theory—if we look for confirmations.
(2) Confirmations should count only if they are the result of risky predictions; that is to say, if, unenlightened by the theory in question, we should have expected an event which was incompatible with the theory—an event which would have refuted the theory.
(3) Every 'good' scientific theory is a prohibition; it forbids certain things to happen. The more a theory forbids, the better it is.
(4) A theory which is not refutable by any conceivable event is non-scientific. Irrefutability is not a virtue of a theory (as people often think) but a vice.
(5) Every genuine *test* of a theory is an attempt to falsify it, or to refute it. Testability is falsifiability; but there are degrees of testability: some theories are more testable, more exposed to refutation, than others; they take, as it were, greater risks.
(6) Confirming evidence should not count *except when it is the result of a genuine test of the theory*; and this means that it can be presented as a serious but unsuccessful attempt to falsify the theory. (I now speak in such cases of 'corroborating evidence'.)
(7) Some genuinely testable theories, when found to be false, are still upheld by their admirers—for example by introducing *ad hoc* some auxiliary assumption, or by re-interpreting the theory *ad hoc* in such a way that it escapes refutation. Such a procedure is always possible, but it rescues the theory from refutation only at the price of destroying, or at least lowering, its scientific status. (I later described such a rescuing operation as a '*conventionalist twist*' or a '*conventionalist stratagem*'.)[4]

These ideas gave rise to what Popper would later call 'the falsifiability criterion of demarcation'.

The Falsifiability Criterion

Popper called the problem of demarcation 'Kant's problem', but his discussions of it more often refer to the verifiability criterion of meaning proposed by Wittgenstein and the logical positivists. According to this criterion, a statement is both meaningful and scientific if-and-only-if it is analytic or empirically verifiable. Wittgenstein and the positivists hoped that their criterion would 'eliminate' metaphysical statements as literally meaningless 'pseudo-statements'. But Popper thought that it had serious problems of its own. It failed as a theory of science because it could not, due to the problem of induction, account for the scientific character of scientific laws and theories, which, as strictly universal statements, cannot be verified by experience. But it also failed as a theory of meaning and—since it was neither analytically true nor empirically verifiable—was not even meaningful according to its own criterion.

Here Popper had a profoundly simple insight. He realized that there is an asymmetry between the verifiability and the falsifiability of the strictly universal laws and theories of empirical science. Universal statements have the logical form '*All S's are P's*', where *S* is a subject term and *P* is a predicate term. Their contradictories are existential statements with the logical form '*Some S's are not P's*'. Popper recognized that the strictly universal theories and laws of empirical science, which quantify over infinite or indeterminate domains, cannot be verified by any finite number of existential statements. This is the problem of induction. But he also recognized that a strictly universal theory can be refuted, or *falsified*, by just one genuine counter-example. This asymmetry means that neither verifiability nor falsifiability can serve as a criterion of meaning without violating the logical principle that the negation of a meaningful statement is itself a meaningful statement. But it also means that falsifiability might succeed as a criterion of demarcation where verifiability had failed. Popper proposed that we should 'interpret natural laws or theories as genuine statements which are *partially decidable, i.e.* which are, for logical reasons, not verifiable but, *in an asymmetrical way, falsifiable only*: they are statements which are tested by being submitted to systematic attempts to falsify them'.[5] He thus proposed that falsifiability, and not verifiability, is what distinguishes empirical science from metaphysics. In order for a system of statements to be scientific in the empirical sense, its logical form must 'be such that it can be singled out, by means of empirical tests, in a negative sense: it must be possible for an empirical scientific system to be refuted by experience'.[6]

Scientists, according to Popper, cannot discover and justify their theories by generalizing observations. But they can *invent* their theories as speculative solutions to their problems—and then test them against observation and experience:

> In this way, the recognition of unilaterally decidable statements allows us to solve not only the problem of induction (note that there is only one type of argument which proceeds in an inductive direction: the deductive *modus tollens*), but also the more fundamental problem of demarcation, a problem which has given rise to almost all the other problems of epistemology. For our criterion of falsifiability distinguishes with sufficient precision the theoretical systems of the empirical sciences from those of metaphysics (and from conventionalist and tautological systems), without asserting the meaninglessness of metaphysics (which from a historical point of view can be seen to be the source from which the theories of the empirical sciences spring).
>
> Varying and generalizing a well-known remark of Einstein's, one might therefore characterize the empirical sciences as follows: *In so far as a scientific statement speaks about reality, it must be falsifiable: and in so far as it is not falsifiable, it does not speak about reality.*[7]

The falsifiability criterion thus characterizes scientific research as both empirical and rational. It is empirical because we *test* theories against observation and experience. And it is rational because we use the valid argument forms of deductive logic, especially the *modus tollens*, to criticize theories that contradict observation statements that we think are true—and because we never conclude from the fact that a theory has survived our tests that it has been shown to be true. This idea offers a real alternative to inductivism. But in order to understand it, we must think of knowledge and of rationality in a way that does not presuppose that our knowledge must be justified in order to be rational. It is, for this reason, often misunderstood.

How Not to Understand Falsifiability

A lot has been written about falsifiability, and much of it distorts the idea. Falsifiability is thus often misrepresented as a criterion of meaning that is intended, like the positivists' verifiability criterion of meaning, to 'eliminate' metaphysics as meaningless. This idea can be disposed with at once. For Popper, from his earliest publications on the subject, drew a sharp distinction between a criterion of meaning and his criterion of demarcation. He had no interest whatsoever in stating the conditions under which a sentence should be regarded as meaningful. And he believed, as we have already seen, that metaphysical theories may be both meaningful and true, that they are often the source from which scientific theories spring, and that we can argue meaningfully about them despite the fact that we cannot test their truth against empirical observations.

This idea—*that metaphysical statements may be meaningful and true*—also disposes of another confusion, which is often reflected in the 'criticism' that the falsifiability criterion is not itself falsifiable. This charge would be damning *if Popper proposed falsifiability—as the positivists proposed verifiability—as a criterion of meaning, or if he proposed it as a scientific theory.* But Popper did not propose falsifiability as a criterion of meaning. And he was the first to point out that it is not a scientific theory, but a normative proposal about what we should and should not regard as scientific.

These misconceptions confuse Popper's project to state the conditions under which a theory should be regarded as scientific with the positivists' project to 'eliminate' metaphysics as meaningless. So it is important to point out that falsifiability, according to Popper, does not apply to individual statements, but to *systems* of statements. This marks an important departure from the verifiability criterion, which, as a criterion of meaning, applied to individual statements. If falsifiability were a criterion of meaning, then any individual statement that was not itself falsifiable could not be regarded as scientific. But falsifiability is not a criterion of meaning. And it is not necessary, according to Popper, that each and every consequence of a theory be falsifiable in order for that theory to be regarded scientific. It will suffice, on the contrary, if we can find just one logical consequence of a theoretical system that admits of empirical test.

Still, some critics say that falsifiability suffers from the same epistemological problems as verifiability. 'It is impossible to prove that a theory is true by observation or experiment', these critics say, 'but it is just as impossible to prove that a theory is false by these methods'. This criticism stems partly from the fact that Popper held that observation statements that can falsify a theory are not themselves justified by experience. But it also stems from the fact that the predictions that can be deduced to test a theory are typically derived not from a universal theory alone, but from that theory in conjunction with statements of initial conditions and other auxiliary assumptions. If such a prediction is false, then it may well be one of these other statements, and not the theory itself, that is really to blame.

The upshot, according to these critics, is that the apparent asymmetry between falsification and verification is merely apparent. Falsifications, like verifications, are never conclusive. So the falsificationist and the inductivist are really in the same epistemological boat.

Now it is true that the observation statements that falsify theories are not themselves justified, that theories are typically not falsified in isolation but only in conjunction with other statements, and that no falsification is or ought to be regarded as conclusive. But citing these facts as 'criticisms' also betrays a misunderstanding of Popper's view. For these are not problems with falsifiability, according to Popper, but an integral part of the idea itself. Falsifications, for Popper, are *never* conclusive or final. For it is always possible to reexamine the empirical evidence, and to find that we are mistaken about it. Falsifying observation statements, like theories, are always conjectural in nature. And it follows that our refutations, like our conjectures, are *always* tentative and subject to revision.

Here it may seem as if the falsificationist and the inductivist really are in the same boat. Popper, however, wrote that 'the deductive method of testing cannot establish or justify the statements which are being tested; nor is it intended to do so'.[8] And he emphasized the point with regard to falsification:

In point of fact, no conclusive disproof of a theory can ever be produced; for it is always possible to say that the experimental results are not reliable, or that the discrepancies which are asserted to exist between the experimental results and the theory are only apparent and that they will disappear with the advance of our understanding.[9]

And again:

We say that a theory is falsified only if we have accepted basic statements which contradict it. This condition is necessary, but not sufficient; for we have seen that non-reproducible single occurrences are of no significance to science. Thus a few stray basic statements contradicting a theory will hardly induce us to reject it as falsified. We shall take it as falsified only if we discover a reproducible effect which refutes the theory.[10]

The so-called 'basic statements' that report our observations and that falsify or corroborate a theory, in particular, are not themselves justified by our observations, but accepted or rejected by *decisions* that can always be reevaluated:

20

Every test of a theory, whether resulting in its corroboration or falsification, must stop at some basic statement or other which we *decide to accept*. If we do not come to any decision, and do not accept some basic statement or other, then the test will have led nowhere. But considered from a logical point of view, the situation is never such that it compels us to stop at this particular basic statement rather than at that, or else give up the test altogether. For any basic statement can again in its turn be subjected to tests, using as a touchstone any of the basic statements which can be deduced from it with the help of some theory, either the one under test, or another. This procedure has no natural end. Thus if the test is to lead us anywhere, nothing remains but to stop at some point or other and say that we are satisfied, for the time being.[11]

Here, the point to be made is that there is no 'mechanical procedure' in Popper's view either for making conjectures or for rejecting them. The basic statements that may or may not contradict a theory cannot be justified by observations and are, from a logical point of view, accepted or rejected by 'free decisions'.[12] But this means no more and no less than that the acceptance or rejection of an observation statement or a theory requires judgment and discretion. The fact that a falsifying basic statement does not contradict a theory in isolation, but a long conjunction of assumptions, including so-called 'background knowledge' that we may not even be able to fully articulate, means that any or all of the statements in this conjunction may be responsible for the conflict, and that we may differ regarding what its supposed truth should be taken to refute. The element of decision, or choice, is thus fundamental to Popper's understanding of falsifiability.

But what about the asymmetry between falsifiability and verifiability? Are the falsificationist and the inductivist really in the same epistemological boat?

The falsificationist and the inductivist are clearly in the same epistemological boat if, by that, we mean the boat of uncertainty. *Everybody*, according to Popper, seems to be in *that* boat. But this too is a distortion of his view. For Popper *begins* with the idea that all of our scientific knowledge is fallible and uncertain. The issue for him is not whether science is certain, but whether and how it is objective and rational. And here, the point to be made is that their epistemological boats are very different when it comes to objectivity and rationality, and that the asymmetry between falsification and verification remains firmly in place.

21

There are no such things as conclusive falsifications because human beings are fallible and may always be mistaken in thinking that a basic statement is true, or in thinking that a false prediction means that it is our theory, as opposed to one of our auxiliary assumptions, that is to blame. But there are no such things as conclusive verifications because the inductive inferences by which observations would verify theories are *invalid*. The issue again is not certainty, but objectivity and rationality. Valid arguments are not conclusive because we may always be mistaken about their premises. But invalid arguments are not conclusive because their conclusions *do not even follow* from their premises. This means that they may be false *even if all of their premises are true*. The upshot is that we can regard them as justifying their conclusions only by taking a subjective and irrational leap. There can be no doubt that such leaps may be motivated by observation. But there can also be no doubt that they go beyond the evidence, and that there is no contradiction in asserting all of the premises of an inductive argument and denying that its conclusion is true. This is the asymmetry between falsification and verification. If our knowledge of basic statements were infallible, then a true falsifying basic statement would conclusively falsify the conjunction consisting of the theory under test, the statement of its initial conditions, and our background knowledge. It is true that this would not tell us that the theory that we were testing is false. But it would tell us that *something* in our theoretical system is mistaken, and it would force us to try to eliminate the error in order to avoid contradicting ourselves. But the situation is entirely different with an inductive argument. Infallible knowledge of its premises is not enough to verify the conclusion of an inductive argument, because the conclusion of an inductive argument does not follow from its premises at all.

I can, perhaps, put the matter in an entirely different way. Deductive arguments can *never* show that their conclusions are true. The most that they can do is to present us with a choice. Either the conclusion derived from the premises of a deductively valid argument is true, or some of the premises from which we derive it are false. This is not proof but choice. The value of the argument is that it clarifies the alternatives between which we must choose if we wish not to contradict ourselves. But it cannot make the choice for us, and it cannot force us to avoid contradictions.

But why can't inductivists say, à la Popper, that 'nothing remains but to stop at some point or other and say that we are satisfied, for the time being'?

Popper would not object were this all that inductivists want to say. Inductivists, however, typically want to say much more: not merely that they are satisfied with their theory, but that their theory is *justified* by the evidence and that its justification makes it objective and rational—*and that you must accept it too.*

Popper's appeal to empirical test, and to deductive logic as the organon of criticism, goes a long way toward explaining how he thought unjustified scientific theories can be regarded as objective and rational. But in the next chapter, I will try to explain a part of his later philosophy that even his most ardent admirers find difficult to accept: his theory of 'epistemology without a knowing subject', 'World 3', and 'the objective mind'.

Endnotes

[1] This is the English title of the first book that Popper wrote, *Die beiden Grundprobleme der Erkenntnistheorie*, which was published only in 1979. His *Logik der Forschung* was an abridged version of this work.

[2] Karl Popper, *Conjectures and Refutations*, Routledge & Kegan Paul, London, 1963. Reprinted by Routledge, London, 1991, p. 33.

[3] Popper, *Conjectures and Refutations*, p. 35.

[4] Popper, *Conjectures and Refutations*, pp. 36-7.

[5] Karl R. Popper, 'A Criterion of the Empirical Character of Theoretical Systems', *Erkenntnis*, **3**, no. 4-6. Reprinted in Popper, *The Logic of Scientific Discovery*, Hutchinson, London, 1959. Reprinted by Routledge, London and New York, 1992, p. 313.

[6] Popper, *The Logic of Scientific Discovery*, p. 41.

[7] Popper, 'A Criterion of the Empirical Character of Theoretical Systems', p. 314.

[8] Popper, *The Logic of Scientific Discovery*, p. 47.

[9] Popper, *The Logic of Scientific Discovery*, p. 50.

[10] Popper, *The Logic of Scientific Discovery*, p. 86.

[11] Popper, *The Logic of Scientific Discovery*, p. 104.

[12] See Popper, *The Logic of Scientific Discovery*, p. 109.

3

Objective Knowledge

I have, thus far, explained Popper's reasons for thinking that we cannot rationally justify our knowledge, and his solutions to the problems of induction and demarcation. These ideas are the germ of his account of how unjustified knowledge can be rational and objective. But they are not the whole story. Popper wrote that:

> Traditional epistemology has studied knowledge or thought in a subjective sense—in the sense of the ordinary usage of the word 'I know' or 'I am thinking'. This, I assert, has led students of epistemology into irrelevances: while intending to study scientific knowledge, they studied in fact something which is of no relevance to scientific knowledge. For *scientific knowledge* simply is not knowledge in the sense of the ordinary usage of the words 'I know'. While knowledge in the sense of 'I know' belongs to what I call the 'second world', the world of *subjects*, scientific knowledge belongs to the third world, to the world of objective theories, objective problems, and objective arguments.[1]

Traditional epistemology has studied the conditions under which a person, or *subject*, is justified in claiming to know that his beliefs are true. But scientific knowledge has nothing to do with whether or not a *person* is justified in claiming to know that his beliefs are true. Whether or not Einstein was justified in believing $E=MC^2$ is irrelevant to science if there is no way to justify $E=MC^2$ itself. And if there were a way to justify $E=MC^2$ itself, then science would be concerned entirely with its justification and not with whether Einstein was justified in believing it.

This is what Popper meant when he said that scientific knowledge is knowledge in the objective sense:

24

Knowledge in this objective sense is totally independent of any-body's claim to know; it is also independent of anybody's belief, or disposition to assent; or to assert, or to act. Knowledge in the objective sense is knowledge without a knower: it is knowledge without a knowing subject.[2]

But in order to explain it, I will need to say a bit more about his anti-psychologism—and I will also need to explain his theory of the three worlds and, in particular, his idea that scientific knowledge belongs to an objective 'World 3'.

Logic and Psychology

Traditional epistemology regards rational knowledge as justified true belief. But the term 'belief' has both logical and psychological meanings. For it may refer either to the logical content of belief—to a proposition or statement that someone believes—or to a person's psychological act or state of believing it. Similar remarks may be made about the terms 'thought', 'idea', and, indeed, 'knowledge' itself. This observation led Popper—like Frege, Bolzano, and Plato before him—to distinguish between our subjective, or *psychological*, thought processes and their objective, or *logical*, contents:

The psychological	The logical
Subjective thought *processes*, or acts of thinking, or thoughts in the subjective sense.	Objective thought *contents*, or contents of acts of thinking, or thoughts in the objective sense.

Epistemologies that focus upon the logical sense of these terms may be called '*objective*'. They are concerned with the objects that we know. Epistemologies that focus upon the psychological sense of these terms may, on the other hand, be called '*subjective*'. They are concerned with subjects who know them.

Popper did not think that there is anything problematic or improper about the psychological senses of these terms, or about knowledge in the subjective sense. He thought, on the contrary, that we obviously have subjective knowledge. But he thought that *scientific* knowledge is knowledge in the objective sense. And he also thought that it is *not* a species of justified true belief.

25

It is also important, insofar as this is concerned, to understand that these ambiguities give rise to two very different 'justified true belief' theories of knowledge, which differ both with regard to what we are trying to justify when we try to justify a belief, and with regard to what counts as a justification of it. For according to the objective theory, we are trying to justify a *statement* or *proposition*. But according to the subjective theory, we are trying to justify a person's *act of believing* a statement or proposition.

Justification in objective epistemology is concerned with showing that a statement is true. But justification in subjective epistemology is concerned with showing that someone acted properly in believing that a statement is true. It is easy, if we confuse these things, to also confuse our belief that a statement is true with truth itself.

Thus, Descartes recognized that a statement and a person's act of believing a statement are two different things. But he regarded the clarity and distinctness of our ideas as the criterion of their truth, and he made the justification of a statement or theory a condition for the justification of our act of believing it. Descartes said that a statement is true if it is clear and distinct, and that a person acts properly in believing a statement only if the statement that he believes is clear and distinct. He said that 'if I hold off from making a judgment when I do not perceive with sufficient clarity and distinctness what is in fact true, I clearly would be acting properly'—but that if I make a judgment, 'and in so doing happen upon the truth by accident, I would still not be without fault'.[3] Descartes no doubt wanted objective truth. But he thought of knowledge entirely in the subjective sense.

Traditional epistemology's failure to distinguish the objective and subjective senses of 'knowledge', together with its idea that the rationality of a belief depends upon its justification, is at the root of a good deal of epistemological confusion, and perhaps even at the root of inductivism itself. We are led by apparently sound arguments to the conclusion that we cannot justify the truth of statements and theories. But we believe that *we* ourselves are rational in believing them. Since we believe that we are rational, we conclude that we are justified. And since we believe that we are justified, we conclude that the statements that we believe must be justified too.

Hume thus thought that we cannot rationally infer from our past experience that the sun will rise tomorrow. But he also thought that we would be crazy to believe otherwise. It is easy to see, if we distinguish between knowledge in the objective sense and knowledge in the subjective sense, that both of these propositions might be true. But the question whether a scientist is crazy or sane should play no role in the evaluation of his theory.

In Chapter 1 I spoke of psychologism as the idea that statements can be justified by experiences. But we can also speak of psychologism as the idea that there is no distinction between being true and being believed to be true—or between the justification of a statement and the justification of a person who believes it. Popper was an opponent of psychologism in each of these senses. He rejected the idea that we can logically justify, or show, that an empirical statement or theory is true. But he nonetheless argued that scientific knowledge is knowledge in the objective sense. This is partly because he thought that science is concerned with whether a *theory* is true, and not with whether a *person* has acted properly in believing it. But it is also because he thought that scientific knowledge belongs to World 3.

The Three Worlds

Popper held that we can distinguish at least three different worlds of human experience.[4] There is, first of all, the world of material objects, such as tables and chairs, trees and plants, planets and stars. This is his World 1. It is objective because material objects can be experienced by others, and autonomous because their existence does not depend upon our own. Then there is the world of mental states, such as pleasures and pains, loves and hates, beliefs and dispositions. This is his World 2. It is subjective because the mental states of one person cannot be experienced by another, and nonautonomous because their existence depends upon the existence of the mind that actually experiences them. There are, however, other things that we experience that do not fit easily into either of these worlds. There are, for example, words and statements, books and symphonies, states and laws, numbers and triangles. And there are, of course, theories, problems, and arguments. These things are immaterial,[5] unlike the objects of World 1. But they are also objective, unlike the mental states of World 2. And when it comes to autonomy, their status seems entirely different. For Popper thought that they are all *produced* by human minds, and that they give rise, once they are created, to consequences that their creators neither intended nor foresaw. These are the objects of World 3.

The objects in Popper's worlds 1, 2, and 3 not only exist, they also interact. This is implicit in his idea that World 3 objects are things that we make. Popper thought that we *create* a World 3 object when we take one of our World 2 thoughts and articulate it in a medium—such as language or music or film—that others can grasp and understand.

We are able, in this way, to treat a thought as an object. We can throw it out onto a table, like a wristwatch or a radio, and take it apart to see how it works. More important—*since a World 3 thought may also be false*—we can see why it doesn't work, or how it could work better. And we are also able to work on improving it until it does. This means that we not only can contribute to World 3, but that we can also work toward improving both our own contributions and the contributions that others have made.

This, in fact, is what I am doing as I write this book. I have some thoughts in mind. But you cannot know what they are so long as I keep them only in mind. Nor can you judge whether or not they are true. So I write them down. And I read over what I have written. In some cases I decide that what I have written is not really what I wanted to say. So I change it, and start all over again. The book that you will eventually read will thus be one of my contributions to World 3. It will, when I have finished writing it, hopefully consist of sentences that express more or less what I think. But even then, when I have finished writing it, I am sure that someone, either myself or someone else, might still convince me otherwise.

So our minds can act upon World 3, and World 3 can act upon our minds. And in this way, our conscious selves can develop and become what they become by contributing to World 3 and by learning from the contributions that others make. Thus, none of us were born into this world knowing about Popper and his philosophy. But the interesting thing is that we can decide, knowing virtually nothing more than his name, to learn something about him and his philosophy—and to transform ourselves into something other than what we are by doing so. We can, in this way, even talk about our conscious selves—which he regarded as the highest stage of development in World 2—as being, to a large extent, products of World 3.

World 3	logical (linguistic) products
↕	↕
World 2	psychological states

Thus far I have talked about interaction between Worlds 2 and 3. But these worlds also interact directly and indirectly with World 1. Popper thought that our World 2 states, and especially our conscious selves, act as a sort of control system for our bodies—and that our World 3 creations, especially our scientific theories, are a control system for our minds. When you feel a pain, and move away from what you think is causing it, your physical movement results from an interaction between Worlds 1 and 2. And when you read a book, and accept or reject what it says, your mental movement results from an interaction between Worlds 2 and 3. But when you read a book and, accepting what it says, fill the volume inside a wire coil with iron and run an electric current through it, the movement involved results from an interaction between Worlds 1, 2, and 3.

In this way, Worlds 1 and 3 can indirectly interact with each other through the World 2 medium of the human mind.

World 3	logical (linguistic) products
↕	↕
World 2	psychological states
↕	↕
World 1	physical states

There is nothing so mundane as following a recipe to bake a cake. But this simple process illustrates the way in which a World 2 mind can use a World 3 theory to produce a change upon objects in World 1. And it also illustrates the way in which Worlds 1 and 2 can exercise critical control over the objects in World 3. For we might, depending upon how we like that cake, decide to see whether and how the recipe itself can be improved. This simple example provides an analogy for how we work with scientific theories. Our theories give us directions for acting in the real world. And we can test their adequacy by seeing whether or not they bring about their predicted results.

Earlier I said that we create World 3 objects by articulating our World 2 thoughts in a medium that others can understand. World 3, in this way, consists largely of thoughts that are 'embodied' in World 1. This has led some philosophers to think that they can be 'reduced' to the material medium in which they are expressed. But Popper thought that a book is not the paper on which it is written. For it is not the *paper* that we understand when we understand what it says. It is the *thought* itself that we understand, and that we must understand if we are to use it to make changes in the material world.[6]

Thus, where Quine argues for materialism by saying 'The bodily states exist anyway; why add the others?'[7] Popper replies:

I admit that the denial of mental states simplifies matters. For example, the difficult body-mind problem simply disappears, which no doubt is very convenient: it saves us the trouble of solving it. But I do not think that Quine is consistent when he asks 'Why add

29

the others?' To whom does he address this question? To our bodies? Or to our physical states? Or to our behaviour? Quine *argues*. And arguments, I hold, belong to world 3. Arguments may be *understood*, or grasped. And understanding or grasping is a world 2 affair: our bodies can grasp a stone or stick, but they cannot grasp or understand an argument.

Also, I am sure that it is Quine's *intention* (again a world 2 term) to *convince* us by his arguments, or at least to give us something to *think* about (two more world 2 terms).

Clearly he would not be *satisfied* (also a world 2 term) if he would only evoke a certain kind of behaviour in us—let us call it agreeing behaviour—such as the noises 'Exactly!' or 'That is so!' or 'Well done!'[8]

And where materialists suggest that we have good reason to think that their reductionist program will finally succeed, Popper points out that it is really just a promissory note.[9] For we simply do not have many examples of successful and complete reductions even in the physical sciences, where one might expect that reductionism would be more apt to work. But quite aside from this, Popper thought that the proponents of reductionism typically ignore the more serious problems that face it, 'such as the difficulty of reducing to psychology, and then to biology, the ups and downs of the British Trade Deficit and its relations to the British Net National Income'.[10]

Popper introduced his theory of the three worlds as an attempt to solve two different philosophical problems at once: the problem of objective knowledge on the one hand, and the body-mind problem on the other. He thought that these two problems are interrelated, and that 'in order to understand the relationship between the body and the mind, we must first recognize the existence of objective knowledge as an objective and autonomous product of the human mind, and, in particular, the ways in which we use such knowledge as a control system for critical problem-solving'.[11] He conceived of the mind, in this way, as a control system for the body, and of our objective knowledge as a control system for the mind.

I will discuss Popper's solution to the body-mind problem in Chapter 4, and I will say more about the problem of objective knowledge in a moment. But I first want to explain why World 3 is the key to his critical rationalism.

Critical Rationalism

Critical rationalism can be understood, in Popper's own words, as an attitude of admitting that '*I may be wrong and you may be right*', and that '*by an effort, we may get nearer to the truth*'. The effort that he had in mind is the effort of critical discussion. It is the effort by which we discover a problem, propose a theory as its tentative solution, try to eliminate errors that we find in it, and through the elimination of such errors progress to the discovery of a new problem. But here, the very possibility of criticism—at least as Popper envisioned it—depends upon the possibility of contradiction. It depends, in other words, upon there being statements that are related in such a way that they cannot all be true and they cannot all be false. *But there are no statements, and hence no contradictions, in Worlds 1 & 2.* Statements are neither material objects nor mental entities. They are not the material media—the sound waves through which we talk or the paper upon which we write—that we use to express them. But they are objective enough to be experienced by different minds. And they very often have consequences, both logical and otherwise, that their creators neither intended nor foresaw. Statements, in other words, belong to the immaterial but objective World 3. And this, in a nutshell, is why World 3 is the key to critical rationalism.

Knowledge Without a Knowing Subject

Popper, as I have already said, introduced his theory of World 3 in an attempt to solve the problem of objective knowledge. He thought that scientific knowledge belongs to World 3. It is not knowledge in the ordinary sense of the phrase 'I know', but knowledge in the sense of a 'branch of learning; a science; an art'. He thought that traditional epistemology misconceived scientific knowledge as a World 2 state, as the 'state of being aware or informed', and thus focused its attention upon irrelevant problems, such as specifying the conditions under which a person is justified in claiming to know that his beliefs are true.[12] Contrary to this, Popper thought that:

> ...what is relevant for epistemology is the study of scientific problems and problem situations, of scientific conjectures (which I take as merely another word for scientific hypotheses or theories), of scientific discussions, of critical arguments, and of the role played by evidence in arguments; and therefore of scientific journals and books, and of experiments and their evaluation in scientific arguments.[13]

What is relevant, in other words, is the study of the largely autonomous World 3 of objective knowledge.

This is what Popper meant when he said that scientific knowledge is knowledge without a knowing subject. He did not mean that science can do without scientists, or that it could do without their subjective guesses. But he did mean that we can and do have scientific knowledge without their *knowing*:

> Scientists very often do not claim that their conjectures are true, or that they 'know' them in the subjectivist sense of 'know', or that they believe in them. Although in general they do not claim to know, in developing their research programmes they act on the basis of guesses about what is and what is not fruitful, and what line of research promises further results in the third world of objective knowledge. In other words, scientists act on the basis of a guess or, if you like, of a *subjective belief* (for we may so call the subjective basis of an action) concerning what is promising of impending *growth in the third world of objective knowledge.*[14]

Misunderstanding World 3

Popper's theory of World 3 is often confused with Plato's theory of Ideas or with Frege's theory of the *dritte Reich*. There are, of course, some obvious similarities. But there are also important differences. Plato, first of all, regarded Forms, or Ideas, as eternal and immutable objects. Frege regarded senses and thoughts in much the same way. Their third realm objects can be *discovered*, or apprehended, by human beings. But they have an independent existence of their own. Popper, on the other hand, regarded World 3 objects as human inventions. Our scientific problems, theories, and arguments are non-living structures that we produce. They are, in this respect, similar to biological animal products, such as a bird's nest or spider's web or a beaver's dam or the paths that animals make in a forest.

A second, and perhaps more important, difference pertains to their problem situations. Popper, like Plato and Frege, introduced World 3 in order to solve the problem of objective knowledge. But Plato and Frege introduced their theory of eternal and immutable objects to supply the metaphysical scaffolding *for scientific claims to objective certainty.*[15] And Popper, as we have already seen, did not regard scientific knowledge as certain. His problem was not to explain how objective knowledge can be certain. It was to explain how fallible knowledge can be objective. And far from supplying support for claims to certainty, World 3 is introduced to supply the means for criticizing them. Thus, the justified true belief theory of knowledge said that the objectivity of scientific knowledge depends upon whether or not we know it, and that whether or not we know it depends upon whether or not we can justify it. But Popper said that the objectivity of scientific knowledge depends upon our ability to understand and communicate and criticize it. And he introduced World 3 in order to explain how understanding, communication, and criticism are possible.

A third way in which Popper's third world differs from Frege's *dritte Reich* and Plato's world of eternal and immutable Forms is that World 3 objects are subject to evolutionary change through a process that is at once both creative and critical. So World 3 objects are neither eternal nor immutable. And World 3, itself, may grow as we criticize and try to improve upon the contributions that we have made to it.

Popper tried to model this creative and critical process in his so-called 'tetradic schema',

$$P_1 \to TT \to EE \to P_2$$

in which 'P_1' is a problem from which we start; 'TT' is a theory that we tentatively propose to solve it; 'EE' is error elimination, or criticism; and 'P_2' is a new problem that emerges as a result of our criticism. The schema, of course, is an over-simplification, since we typically work with several different problems and theories at once. But Popper introduced it to model the growth of scientific knowledge as a learning process. And it is important to note that belief and justification play no role in it at all. The schema, on the contrary, emphasizes the role that problems play in scientific inquiry, and the fact that scientific inquiry and human learning in general are open-ended and never-ending processes of change. But it also gives a good account of how we come to understand World 3 objects themselves.

Understanding World 3

Epistemic logic focuses upon the analysis of such linguistic formulations as 'S knows p' or 'S knows that p', and 'S believes p' or 'S believes that p'—in which 'S' stands for a person, subject, or scientist; and 'p' for a proposition, theory, or state or affairs that S knows or believes to be true. Subjective epistemology is an attempt to specify the conditions under which a person is justified in claiming to know that his beliefs are true, and objective epistemology is an attempt to specify the conditions under which a theory itself is justified as true. Popper, however, thought that this kind of analysis has nothing to do with scientific knowledge. For a scientist, according to Popper, 'neither knows nor believes'.[16] What does a scientist do? Popper offered the following list:

> '*S* tries to understand *p*.'
> '*S* tries to think of alternatives to *p*.'
> '*S* tries to think of criticisms of *p*.'
> '*S* proposes an experimental test for *p*.'
> '*S* tries to axiomatize *p*.'
> '*S* tries to derive *p* from *q*.'
> '*S* tries to show that *p* is not derivable from *q*.'
> '*S* proposes a new problem *x* arising out of *p*.'
> '*S* proposes a new solution of the problem *x* arising out of *p*.'
> '*S* criticizes his latest solution of the problem *x*.'[17]

This list can be extended at length. But the activities that it mentions are different from '*S* knows *p*' or '*S* believes *p*' or even '*S* doubts *p*'. Many of these activities appeal to logic and logical arguments. But there is no mention of the use of such arguments to justify scientific theories, or to try to establish them either as true or as probably true. The list, on the contrary, mentions creative and critical activities that may help us to *understand* a scientific theory and the problems that it is supposed to solve. And while it is customary to suppose that scientists might want to criticize theories that they doubt or believe to be false, Popper, in commenting on these activities, emphasized that 'it is quite an important point that we may doubt without criticizing, and criticize without doubting'.[18]

Popper thought that understanding a World 3 object is both a critical and a creative process, and he tried to explain it in terms of making, or remaking, the object itself:

> According to my view, we may understand the grasping of a World 3 object as an active process. We have to explain it as the making, the re-creation, of that object. In order to understand a difficult Latin sentence, we have to construe it: to see how it is made, and to re-construct it, to re-make it. In order to understand a *problem*, we have to try at least some of the more obvious solutions, and to discover that they fail; thus we rediscover that there is a difficulty—a problem. In order to understand a *theory*, we have first to understand the problem which the theory was designed to solve, and to

see whether the theory does better than do any of the more obvious solutions. In order to understand a somewhat difficult argument like Euclid's proof of the theorem of Pythagoras (there are simpler proofs of this theorem), we have to do the work ourselves, taking full note of what is assumed without proof. In all these cases, understanding becomes "intuitive" when we have acquired the feeling that we can do the work of reconstruction at will, at any time.[19]

Objectivity, Rationality, and the Third World

Dogmatism and psychologism were characteristic of the 'classical' rationalist and empiricist versions of justificationist epistemology—and if there really were foundations that *everyone* agreed to be self-evident, clear and distinct, and indubitable, then no one would have worried too much about them. The problem, however, was that justificationists differed not only with regard to their foundations, but also with regard to their criteria for recognizing them. And *this* simple disagreement between dogmatism and psychologism was itself enough to refute classical foundationalism.

We have, in this chapter, focused upon Popper's idea of objective knowledge and his theory of World 3. But I want to end with just a word about their consequences for rationality.

Foundationalists equate the rationality of scientific knowledge with its logical justification:

$$rationality = justification = logic$$

where 'logic' may refer to either deductive or inductive arguments. Popper, of course, rejects this justificationist theory of rationality along with justificationism itself. He equates rationality with logical criticism instead:

$$rationality = criticism = logic$$

where 'logic' refers to only deductive arguments.

Criticism, for Popper, is a World 3 process that deals with World 3 objects. We criticize a *statement* by trying to show that some of its *logical consequences* are *false*. Criticism thus attempts to show that a *theory* is *false* by showing that it is *inconsistent*—either with itself, or with other *statements* that we hold to be true.

But here, it is important to understand that *with the exception of contradictions, logic alone cannot show that a statement is false.*

35

If two statements are contradictory, then one must be true and the other false. But this is not enough to tell us *which* is true and *which* is false. And *since no statement can be justified* (or shown to be true), it follows that the acceptance or rejection of criticism always involves a World 2 *judgment.*

It follows from this that *reason cannot compel belief.*

Rationality, according to Popper, is not so much a property of knowledge as a task for humans. What is rational is not so much the content of a theory or a belief as the way in which we hold it.

We are rational to the extent to which we are open to criticism, including self-criticism; and to the extent to which we are willing to change our beliefs when confronted with what we judge to be good criticism.

We are, in short, rational to the extent to which we are willing to appeal to reasons and arguments, as opposed to violence and force, to resolve our disputes.

I will return to this idea of rationality in Chapter 9, when I discuss Popper's views about open society. But the next chapter will focus upon World 2 and Popper's solution to the body-mind problem.

Endnotes

[1] Karl R. Popper, *Objective Knowledge*, revised edition, Oxford University Press, New York, 1979, p. 108.

[2] Popper, *Objective Knowledge*, p. 109.

[3] René Descartes, *Meditations on First Philosophy*, originally published in 1641, translated from the Latin by Donald A. Cress, Hackett, Cambridge, 1979, p. 38.

[4] This is a rough grained distinction. We could, if we liked, distinguish between many more worlds than three. But we cannot, without stretching our concepts beyond recognition and any useful function, say that only matter or mind exist.

[5] Though some of them, e.g., books, are embodied in material objects.

[6] This is Popper's main argument for the existence of the mental world:

My main argument for the existence of the world 2 of subjective experiences is that we must normally grasp or understand a world 3 theory before we can use it to act upon world 1; but grasping or understanding a theory is a mental affair, a world 2 process: my view is that world 3 usually interacts with world 1 *via* the mental world 2. (Karl Popper, 'Indeterminism is not enough' in *ENCOUNTER* 40, 1973, pp. 20-26.)

[7] W.V.O. Quine, *Word and Object*, The M.I.T. Press, Cambridge, 1960, p. 264. Quoted in Karl R. Popper, *Knowledge and the Body-Mind Problem*, edited by M.A. Notturno, Routledge, London, 1994, p. 8.

[8] Popper, *Knowledge and the Body-Mind Problem*, pp. 8-9.

[9] See Karl R. Popper and John C. Eccles, *The Self and Its Brain*, Springer International, New York, 1977, pp. 96-8.

[10] Popper and Eccles, *The Self and Its Brain*, p. 18.

[11] Popper, *Knowledge and the Body-Mind Problem*, p. ix.

[12] Popper, *Objective Knowledge*, p. 110. Popper cites these entries for 'Knowledge' in *The Oxford English Dictionary* as, respectively, objectivist (World 3) and subjectivist (World 2) senses of the term.

[13] Popper, *Objective Knowledge*, p. 111.

[14] Popper, *Objective Knowledge*, p. 111.

[15] This is how Plato used his theory of Ideas in the fourth century B.C., and it is how Frege used his theory of the *dritte Reich* at the beginning of the twentieth century. Rightly impressed by the subjectivity and fallibility of sense-experience, but still believing in objectively certain knowledge, Plato and Frege each introduced a third realm of eternal and immutable objects, and then insisted that true knowledge involves the apprehension of these objects through an act of the intellect that carries its justification within itself.

[16] Popper, *Objective Knowledge*, p. 141.

[17] Popper, *Objective Knowledge*, pp. 141-2.

[18] Popper, *Objective Knowledge*, p. 142.

[19] Popper and Eccles, *The Self and Its Brain*, p. 44.

4

Knowledge
and the Body-Mind Problem

Scientific psychology has generally ignored the study of consciousness and the thinking self. This, to a large extent, is due to the influence of justificationism, which in its positivist version dismissed talk of non-reducible mental events and conscious selves as unverifiable nonsense. Popper, as we have already seen, regarded the reductionist program in psychology as an improbable promissory note. He argued instead that consciousness evolved as an emergent property of World 1, and conscious selves as emergent properties of World 2. Popper described World 3 as a product of the human mind. But he also thought that World 2 is anchored in World 3, and that our minds, or our selves, cannot exist without it.[1] Indeed, his 'main argument' for the existence of World 2 subjective experiences is that we must normally grasp or understand a World 3 theory before we can use it to act upon World 1.[2] Here, the obvious question is 'How can World 3 be a product of the human mind, if the mind itself cannot exist without it?' But Popper argued that 'our selves, the higher functions of language, and World 3 have all evolved and emerged together, in constant interaction'.[3] In the last chapter I said that Popper introduced his theory of the three worlds partly in an attempt to solve the body-mind problem. In this chapter I will explain how his solution works. But it is important to recognize that Popper did not attempt to *prove* that consciousness exists, or that the mind cannot be reduced to physical states. He *assumed* that this is true and focused instead upon explaining how the body and mind interact. His explanation is entirely speculative. But it does address the problem. For the inability to explain mind-body interaction is the primary objection to mind-body dualism. And far from rejecting dualism, Popper appealed to World 3 to explain how bodies and minds interact.

38

Popper's theory, in a nutshell, is that animal consciousness evolved as a control system for the body; that World 3 evolved as a *plastic* control system for the mind; and that human consciousness evolved with the higher linguistic functions that distinguish human beings from other conscious animals. The problems of survival are the catalyst for this evolution. And Worlds 2 and 3 evolve as attempts to solve the ever-evolving problems that confront animals living in World 1.

An Evolutionary Approach

Popper's theory of evolution is based upon his tetradic schema,

$$P_1 \rightarrow TT \rightarrow EE \rightarrow P_2$$

in which 'P_1', again, is a problem; 'TT' is a trial solution to P_1; 'EE' is an attempt to eliminate errors in TT; and 'P_2' is a new problem that emerges as a result. Popper thought that this schema, which emphasizes the *activity* of an animal in responding to problems in its environment, can explain emergent evolution, or the emergence of something entirely new. Thus:

> P_1 may be due to the slow drying up of large pools containing fish. This may pose for the individual fish a problem of insufficient supply of food within the pool in which the fish finds itself. Then TT may consist in a changed behaviour of this fish. For example, the organism in question may invent a new behavioural *aim*: the aim of getting from one pool to another over dry land. With it, it invents a new problem P_2: *how* to get from one pool to another. P_1 was the problem of how to get food. P_2 is the problem of how to get over dry land. It is clear that these two problems are completely different—qualitatively different.
>
> Thus P_2 may be an entirely new problem—one that has never before arisen (although it may arise in stages)—while P_1 was a very old problem, that of getting enough food.[4]

These problem situations cannot be reduced to World 1, or to World 2. They instead *emerge* as a fish strives to survive in its environment.

Popper thought that problems provide the catalyst for evolution. He thought that all of life is problem solving, and that living things—at both the individual and species levels—are constantly confronted with problems of survival and are actively engaged in trying to solve them. He thought that individuals solve their problems by trying out new patterns of behavior, and that species solve their problems by trying out new genetic patterns—or mutations—in the breeding of individuals. But here, changes in behavioral aims may lead to changes in behavioral dispositions, and changes in behavioral dispositions may favor some mutations and anatomical changes over others:

> According to our schema, new behavioural aims, such as getting over land into another pool, will be followed by new *skills*—and these may become *traditional* in a population of fish. If they do, then those anatomic mutations that make it even slightly easier to practice the new skills will be of immediate advantage. They will be favoured by natural selection.[5]

This example suggests how changes in World 2 can lead to changes in World 1. Here, the fish's behavioral aims and dispositions belong to World 2, and its anatomy—along with its body, the food that it eats, the pool that it lives in, and the dry land that it is trying to cross—belong to World 1. Popper, insofar as this is concerned, argued that the changes in an individual fish's World 2 behavioral aims and dispositions are more important than the changes in its species' genetic instructions. For mutations cannot succeed unless they favor successful behavior patterns that already exist.

But the important point, from our perspective, is that the changes themselves are generated by *problems*, and selected for their success in solving them—and that these problems arise from the relationship between an animal and its environment. Problems of survival, as in the example of the fish, are typical. They do not exist in and of themselves, but instead *emerge* as the fish interacts with its pool. Fish do not seem to have the higher linguistic functions that allow humans to describe the world around us and argue about it. But their survival problems may, nonetheless, be regarded as emergent properties that belong to a primitive World 3. And if we regard them in this way, then we can even say that the evolution of an animal species involves an interaction between Worlds 1, 2, and 3. I will, in what follows, focus our discussion of evolution on Popper's account of how the self, World 3, and the higher functions of language emerge in constant interaction with each other.

Human Consciousness

Popper thought that human consciousness and the self evolve from a primitive state of animal consciousness as the human individual and species attempt to solve their problems of survival. But in order to understand this theory, we will need to introduce his idea of 'genetic dualism' and his distinction between the four functions of language.

Popper thought that evolving animal systems typically display a 'genetic dualism' that closely resembles mind-body dualism itself. We can, in other words, typically distinguish between two parts of an organism, between 'a *behaviour-controlling part* like the central nervous system of the higher animals, and an *executive part* like the sense organs and the limbs'.[6] Genetic dualism is already at work in Popper's account of how World 2 behavioral aims and dispositions can favor World 1 anatomical changes in a species. But it also gives rise to the idea of the mind as a control system for the body. And this, in turn, gives rise to the idea of objective knowledge, by which I mean our World 3 problems and theories, as a control system for the mind. Here, the basic idea is that our World 2 behavioral aims and dispositions can, to some extent, control the World 1 physical states of our bodies; that we can use our World 3 objective knowledge, to some extent, to control the behavioral aims and dispositions of our minds; and that we can, to some extent, measure the evolutionary 'progress' of a species by the sophistication of the control systems that it has grown to solve its problems.

This led Popper to distinguish between four functions of language, the higher of which—the descriptive and critical functions—form the basis for our World 3 objective knowledge.[7]

Higher linguistic functions (basis of World 3)	Argumentative or critical function
	Descriptive or informative function
Lower linguistic functions	Communicative function
	Expressive function

The higher linguistic functions here presuppose the lower ones, but not vice-versa. Thus, an animal may be able to express itself but not communicate, to communicate but not describe; or to describe but not argue. But the argumentative or critical function involves all of the others at once. So if an animal argues, then it describes, communicates, and expresses itself as well. Description and argumentation may, for this reason alone, be regarded as 'higher' linguistic functions. But there are two more important reasons why Popper regarded them as such. The first is that they involve such abstract and sophisticated logical ideas as truth, falsity, validity, and invalidity, which the lower functions alone do not. The second is that they are our most important tools for solving problems.

Now Popper thought that the higher linguistic functions form the basis for World 3, and that the self grows and develops—or *that we become selves*—by interacting with World 3. Thus, a baby, at birth, is at a primitive stage of human development. He cannot yet speak, let alone read or write. So he is not yet able to describe the world around him and argue about it. And he does not yet have 'full consciousness' or a self. But he is conscious, which means that he can, to some extent, sense and respond to the world around him. And he can also express his sensations, and communicate them to others—as he will, no doubt, do as he begins to experience discomfort in his environment. His sensations thus act as a control system for his body as they alert him to the problems in his relationship to the physical world.

The baby may feel hungry or cold—and express his feelings by crying. And his crying, if he is lucky, will communicate his discomfort to his parents and guardians. Here, we can regard his crying both as a natural expression of discomfort and as a primitive attempt to communicate and solve a problem. For the baby is hungry. He cries. His parents come. They feed him—and he no longer feels hungry. His crying may thus be effective. And the baby will resort to it time and again. But it will probably not be very efficient, for he cannot yet describe his problem or criticize the attempts of those around him to solve it. So the people who care for him will have to guess what his problem is, and it may take several trials and errors before they get it right. They may, for example, warm him when he is hungry and feed him when he is cold. And the baby, in most cases, will become better able to solve his problems only as he grows a self: only, that is, as he develops his descriptive and critical linguistic abilities—and full consciousness—by interacting more and more with World 3 and the objective knowledge that is in it.

Here, it is interesting to note that the baby's problem, like the fish's, does not exist in and of itself, but emerges with the relationship between the baby and its environment. A fetus under normal conditions presumably does not feel hungry or cold in the womb, but the baby may once his body is in the world.

problems	World 3
$\updownarrow$	$\updownarrow$
consciousness $\leftrightarrow$ body in world	World 2 $\leftrightarrow$ World 1

It is also interesting to note that the baby's use of his voice does not yet involve an interaction with World 3. We may regard his cries as a primitive use of language. They express his discomfort, and they may communicate it to others. But they do not yet describe it—though they will probably grow louder as his parents try and fail to solve his problem.

World 3:	critical function:	theories
	descriptive function:	statements, myths, stories
World 2:	communicative function:	sensations
	expressive function:	

We can, in this way, see a connection between the lower expressive and communicative linguistic functions, and the World 2 thought processes whose content we have yet to articulate in language. And we can, I think, also see the emergence of problems and World 3.

Full Consciousness and the Self

Popper used the terms 'full consciousness', 'the self', and 'the ego' interchangeably. He wrote that human consciousness 'contains a great many residues of lower forms of consciousness, such as all kinds of vague feelings mingled with more pronounced feelings of pain';[8] but that 'there is no doubt that we achieve full consciousness—or the highest state of consciousness—when we are thinking, especially when we try to formulate our thoughts in the form of statements and arguments'.[9] He thus described the self as a World 2 phenomenon 'anchored' in World 3. He meant that it consists mainly of psychological thought processes and their logical thought contents, and that it is closely linked with human language and objective knowledge. And he thought that the self has an intuitive understanding of World 3 'theories about space and time, about physical bodies in general, about people and their bodies, about our own particular bodies as extending in space and time, and about certain regularities of being awake and being asleep'.[10] He said that the self is a result of placing ourselves into an objective structure that allows us to get a view of ourselves from the outside—and that this view, which is possible only with the help of a descriptive language, is what makes us aware of ourselves, and also of our eventual deaths.

More important, Popper thought that the self serves as a plastic control center for the body, and that the World 3 theories that it understands serve as a plastic control center for the self. This is his solution to the problem of how bodies and minds interact. Simply put, the mind interacts with the body by serving as a control system for its movements. But in order to understand it better, I will need to explain what Popper meant by a 'plastic control'.

Popper wrote that:

In all higher organisms we find a hierarchy of controls. There are controls regulating the heartbeat, the breathing, and the balance of the organism. There are chemical controls and nervous controls. There are controls of healing processes and controls of growth. And in all freely moving animals, there is the central control of the movements of the animal. This control, it appears, is the highest in the hierarchy. I conjecture that mental states are connected with this central and highest control system, and that they help to make this system more plastic. A control like that which makes us blink when something suddenly approaches our eyes I call a 'non-plastic control'. When the possible reactions cover a wide spectrum of possibilities, I speak of a 'plastic control'.[11]

He thought that many of our expressive movements are not consciously controlled, and that there are many others that we have learned so well that they have sunk into the level of unconscious control. But he also thought that the self is able, by its use of the theories in World 3, to exercise 'a plastic control over some of our movements, which, if so controlled, are human actions'.[12]

The self is thus not the highest control center in this hierarchy of controls. It is, on the contrary, itself controlled by World 3 theories. This control, however, is plastic—and, 'like all plastic controls, of the give-and-take, or feedback, type.'[13] For we can—and we do—change our World 3 theories.

Popper articulated this theory in the following three theses:

1. In the evolution of the *species*, the ego or the self or self-consciousness emerges together with the higher functions of language—that is, the descriptive and the argumentative functions—and it interacts with these functions.
2. In the development of the *child*, the ego or self or self-consciousness develops with the higher functions of language, and therefore after the child has learned to express himself,

and to communicate with other persons, and to understand his relations to other persons, and to adjust himself to his physical environment.

3. The self or the ego is linked with the central control function of the brain on the one hand, and it interacts with world 3 objects on the other. In so far as it interacts with the brain, the location of interaction may be anatomically localizable. I suggest that the interaction is centred in the speech centre of the brain.[14]

Popper's idea that the self, or full consciousness, is anchored in World 3 underscores the conception of it as an emergent property of World 2. The self emerges, or comes into existence—along with our higher linguistic abilities and our World 3 thought contents—as we grasp the stories, problems, and theories that other people have articulated, and articulate our own World 2 thoughts in language. This idea also points to a division between our consciousness of bodily sensations, which we may express and communicate to others through the lower linguistic functions, and full consciousness, which involves an individual's use of language to describe the world with statements and theories that are true or false, and to criticize them with logical arguments that are valid or invalid. The self that emerges through this process can then use these World 3 theories as a control system for itself. It can, in other words, use the thought contents that are stored in books and libraries—and, indeed, now also in electronic form on the internet—to direct its own actions. And it can also grow, as World 3 itself grows, as it understands the problems and theories in World 3 and contributes new problems and theories of its own.

Worlds	Contents	Linguistic Functions
3	scientific problems and theories	critical
	myths, stories, theories	descriptive
2	self, ego, full consciousness	critical, descriptive
	sensations, feelings	communicative, expressive
1	body	

Learning to be a Self

Popper's talk about full consciousness may be misleading to the extent to which it suggests a final form of human development. This is already apparent in his tetradic schema, $P_1{\to}TT{\to}EE{\to}P_2$, which, by beginning and ending with problems, indicates that human learning, evolution, and the growth of scientific knowledge are one and all never-ending processes. Earlier I said that Popper thought that the child is not a self at birth. We must, on the contrary, *learn to be* selves.[15] This learning to be a self is an active process in which we learn first to interact with other people, and then with the problems and theories in World 3, until we finally learn to contribute new problems and theories of our own. 'The child learns to know his environment; but persons are the most important objects within his environment; and through their interest in him—and through learning about his own body—he learns in time that he is a person himself.'[16] We thus become selves first by becoming conscious of other people and then by developing theories about them and about our selves:

> Long before we attain consciousness and knowledge of ourselves, we have, normally, become aware of other persons, usually our parents. ... I suggest that a consciousness of self begins to develop through the medium of other persons: just as we learn to see ourselves in a mirror, so the child becomes conscious of himself by sensing his reflection in the mirror of other people's consciousness of himself.[17]

The self, in Popper's view, is not immutable. It is something that comes into being and evolves as we acquire and create objective knowledge. Learning to be a self is thus a gradual life long process with no predetermined end. We create our selves, and recreate our selves over and again, as we recreate the problems and theories in World 3 in order to understand them, and then create and recreate new problems and theories of our own. Full consciousness is, in this way, a life long task. Our selves grow and change, along with our objective scientific knowledge, as we learn more and more about ourselves and about the world around us.

This idea of a freely evolving self may seem attractive. But Popper himself thought that humans have very ambivalent attitudes toward change—that we fear it almost as much as we crave it—and that many of the most influential theories in the history of philosophy have been attempts to relieve our fears either by denying the possibility of change, or by regarding it as predetermined by scientific laws. I will return to this theme in Chapter 7 when I explain the poverty of historicism. But I want first to explore the problem of change in a different context. For Popper thought that the changes in our scientific knowledge are directed by our aim to discover objective and absolute truth. And this idea—objective and absolute truth—has been much maligned in the twentieth century as a result of the collapse of foundationalism. So I want, in the next chapter, to explain Popper's idea that truth is the regulative ideal of science.

Endnotes

[1] See Karl R. Popper, *Knowledge and the Body-Mind Problem*, edited by M.A. Notturno, Routledge, London, 1994, p. 129.

[2] See Karl Popper, 'Indeterminism is not enough' in *ENCOUNTER* 40, 1973, pp. 20-26.

[3] Popper, *Knowledge and the Body-Mind Problem*, p. 129.

[4] Popper, *Knowledge and the Body-Mind Problem*, p. 80.

[5] Popper, *Knowledge and the Body-Mind Problem*, p. 80.

[6] Karl R. Popper, *Objective Knowledge*, revised edition, Oxford University Press, New York, 1979, p. 273.

[7] The figure below can be found in Popper, *Knowledge and the Body-Mind Problem*, p. 84.

[8] Popper, *Knowledge and the Body-Mind Problem*, p. 114.

[9] Popper, *Knowledge and the Body-Mind Problem*, p. 114.

[10] Popper, *Knowledge and the Body-Mind Problem*, pp. 114-15.

[11] Popper, *Knowledge and the Body-Mind Problem*, p. 112.

[12] Popper, *Knowledge and the Body-Mind Problem*, p. 116.

[13] Popper, *Knowledge and the Body-Mind Problem*, p. 115.

[14] Popper, *Knowledge and the Body-Mind Problem*, pp. 131-32.

[15] See Karl R. Popper and John C. Eccles, *The Self and Its Brain*, Springer International, New York, 1977, p. 109.

[16] Popper and Eccles, *The Self and Its Brain*, p. 110.

[17] Popper and Eccles, *The Self and Its Brain*, pp. 109-10.

5

Realism and the Aim of Science

Popper was a metaphysical realist. He thought that the world exists independently of our minds and that statements are true or false independently of what anyone thinks. Popper thought that we can never know with certainty whether or not an empirical theory is true. But he also thought that truth is objective and absolute, and that it is the aim and regulative ideal of scientific inquiry. Science is trying to discover truth. And scientists regulate, or should regulate, their inquiry accordingly. Many philosophers regard the combination of these ideas—that truth is the aim of science, but we can never know whether or when we have discovered it—as problematic. Others regard the ideas that the world exists independently of our minds and that truth is objective and absolute as more problematic still. But these ideas follow directly from the idea that scientific knowledge is fallible. And in this chapter, I will explain how.

In Chapter 1 I said that the collapse of classical foundationalism was due partly to our inability to articulate an objective criterion of truth, and partly to our discovery of serious competitors to Kant's best candidates for *a priori* certain knowledge. The fallibilist philosophy that has emerged from it says that we can never know any theory with certainty, since even our most certain theories may turn out to be false. This idea has led some people to say that there is no truth, and others to say that truth is relative to what we believe. But Popper thought that we can be mistaken only if there is something to be mistaken about—and that we can recognize our mistakes only if we draw a sharp distinction

48

between being-true and being-believed-to-be-true. Any statement that we believe is a statement that we believe to be true. But the fact that we believe that a statement is true is not what makes it true. And it would be impossible to make a mistake if it did. We can, on the contrary, be mistaken about our beliefs only because there are facts independent of our beliefs that make them true or false.

What is Truth?

Popper thought that truth is correspondence with the facts, and that 'an assertion, proposition, statement, or belief, is true if, and only if, it corresponds to the facts'.[1] This idea is as old as Aristotle. But Popper realized that we have to draw a sharp distinction between a criterion of truth and a definition of 'truth' in order to make philosophical sense of it. A criterion of truth states the necessary and sufficient conditions by which we can *determine* whether or not a statement is true. A definition of 'truth' states the necessary and sufficient conditions under which a statement *is* true. The logical positivists said that a definition of 'truth' must include a criterion for determining whether a statement is true.[2] But a *criterion* of truth and a *definition* of 'truth' are two entirely different things. And this becomes clear once we recognize, with fallibilism, that a statement may be true even if we have no way of determining whether or not it is. Popper, insofar as this is concerned, said that we do not have an objective, non-question-begging criterion of truth. But he thought that we nonetheless know what 'truth' means. He was generally critical of the idea that we need to define our terms in order to have a serious discussion. He thought that definitions define terms in terms of other terms, and that the idea that we must define our terms leads to an infinite regress in the same way as the idea that we justify our beliefs. But he also thought that a definition may sometimes help to vindicate our terms against the charge that they are meaningless. And he thought that Alfred Tarski's definition of 'truth' was a vindication in just this sense.

Tarski's definition of 'truth' explains how we can speak about a statement's correspondence to the facts even if we have no criterion for determining whether or not it does. His definition thus specifies the *conditions* under which a statement is true, but it does not include a *criterion* by which we can determine whether or not a statement is true. Tarski said that we can define 'truth' by introducing the idea of a 'metalanguage' in which we can refer both to statements and to the facts to which those statements refer. A metalanguage enables us to assign a name to each and every statement in a language. It thus en-

49

ables us to refer to statements, as opposed to facts, and say that they are true. This can be done in many different ways. But Tarski suggested that the easiest way to do it is to simply enclose a sentence within quotation marks.

Thus, the quotation marks in the statements:

> '*Snow is white*' is true (or corresponds to the facts) if and only if snow is white.

and

> '*Grass is red*' is true if and only if grass is red.

indicate that we are referring to statements—we need to do this in order to say that these statements are true—and not to what the statements themselves refer. These so-called 'T-sentences', or 'Truth-sentences', state the conditions under which the statement in question is true. Thus, the statement 'Snow is white' is true *if* snow is white and *only if* snow is white. And the statement 'Grass is red' is true *if* grass is red and *only if* grass is red. It is important to note that a T-sentence may be true regardless of whether or not the statement to which it refers is true. Thus, most of us would say that 'Grass is red' is a *false* statement. And some people might regard the T-sentence '"*Grass is red*" corresponds to the facts if and only if grass is red' as strange for just this reason. But '"Grass is red" is true if and only if grass is red' states the conditions under which 'Grass is red' is true. We think that the statement 'Grass is red' is false precisely because 'Grass is red' is true *if* grass is red and *only if* grass is red—and because we think that grass, in fact, is *not* red.[3] The truth conditions for any statement that we can think of can, according to Tarski, be stated in just this way. And the complete set of T-sentences for any given language would constitute the definition of 'truth' for that language. It would state the conditions under which each and every statement of that language is true.

All of this may seem too trivial for words. And Popper, in fact, thought that it would be too trivial for words—were it not for the fact that many people think that the term 'truth' is meaningless if we do not have an objective criterion for determining whether or not a statement is true. He said that 'it is decisive to realize that knowing what truth means, or under what conditions a statement is called true, is not the same as, and must be clearly distinguished from, possessing a means of deciding—a *criterion* for deciding—whether a given statement is true or false'.[4] And he frequently quoted Xenophanes as saying:

50

The gods did not reveal, from the beginning,
All things to us; but in the course of time,
Through seeking we may learn, and know things better.

But as for certain truth, no man has known it,
Nor will he know it; neither of the gods,
Nor yet of all the things of which I speak.
And even if by chance he were to utter
The perfect truth, he would himself not know it;
For all is but a woven web of guesses.[5]

But truth is not the only concept for which we have no criterion. Consider our idea of maximization of profit. There are many financial strategies that we can follow. But we have no way of determining whether any of them will maximize our profits. For we can, of course, make great profits without maximizing them. And we may actually maximize our profits while losing money. But maximization of profit is an important regulative ideal for finance—just as truth is an important regulative ideal for science—and we know what it means even if we have no criterion for determining it.

Earlier I said that Popper believed in absolute and objective truth. This is very easily misunderstood, especially if we equate a definition of 'truth' with a criterion of truth. But whether or not truth is absolute has nothing whatsoever to do with whether or not we have a criterion for determining what it is. 'Absolute' simply means that something is not conditional or relative to anything else. Popper thought that truth is absolute in just this sense. Being true is different from being-believed-to-be true. It is not relative to or conditioned by what anyone believes. And it does not depend upon a theory, or evidence, or a historical context, or anything else—except the facts.

But Popper also thought that we can never be absolutely certain whether or not a given statement is true. If we think that a statement is true, then we think that that statement is true. But we need not think that a statement is true in order for it to be true. And our thinking that it is true is no guarantee that we are right. So our knowledge, as opposed to its truth, *is* relative to theory, evidence, historical context, etc., etc. This is what makes our knowledge fallible. But it is also what makes it possible for us to search for truth, and to find it—despite the fact that we can never be absolutely certain whether or not we have actually found it.

Essentialism and Instrumentalism

Popper sometimes explained his own epistemology by contrasting it with *essentialism*, on the one hand, and *instrumentalism*, on the other. It is useful to explore the differences between these theories, because they ultimately turn upon the distinction between a definition of 'truth' and a criterion of truth.

Essentialism, according to Popper, maintains that:

(1) A scientist aims at finding true theories or descriptions of the world that are also explanations of the observable facts;

(2) A scientist can succeed in establishing the truth of such theories beyond any reasonable doubt; and

(3) A truly scientific theory describes 'essences', or the 'essential natures' of things—which are the realities that lie behind the appearances—and theories that describe such essences are final, or 'ultimate', explanations that neither need nor are susceptible to further explanation.

Instrumentalism, on the other hand, holds that:

(4) Prediction, and not explanation, is the real aim of science;

(5) Scientific theories are neither true nor false; and

(6) Scientific theories are not statements but instruments—or, more specifically, computation rules—for making predictions.

The instrumentalist philosophy can be traced to the controversy between Galileo and the Roman Catholic Church. Copernicus had upset the Ptolemaic model of the solar system and contradicted the Bible by saying that the earth revolved around the sun. Galileo upheld the Copernican model as giving a true description of the solar system. But the Church—or, more specifically, Cardinal Bellarmino—argued that the Copernican model is really a 'mathematical hypothesis', or a convenient fiction, for making predictions. The Church forced Galileo to recant his doctrine that the Copernican model is true, and has only recently admitted its error. But the instrumentalist philosophy, under the influence of logical positivism, became popular in the twentieth century due to the general recognition that we do not have an objective criterion for determining whether or not scientific theories are true. The positivists argued that in lieu of such a criterion, scientific theories are best understood as instruments for making predictions.

Now Popper agreed with the essentialists that the aim of science is to find true explanations of the observable facts.[6] But he agreed with the instrumentalists that science can never establish such theories beyond all reasonable doubt, and he argued that there is no reason to think that there is anything like an ultimate explanation that cannot be further explained. Essentialism, he said, impedes scientific inquiry by placing a limit beyond which we can no longer seek an explanation for what we do not understand. But instrumentalism also impedes scientific inquiry by saying that it makes no sense to ask whether or not a scientific theory is really true. Each of these theories confuses the idea of truth with a criterion of truth. And they differ only with regard to whether or not we actually have one.

Popper thought that instrumentalism is right to say that we have no objective criterion of truth and that scientific theories are instruments. But he thought that it is wrong to say that they are *merely* instruments and that science does not aim at truth. He thought that essentialism is right to say that science aims at true explanations, but that it is wrong to say that we can succeed in establishing the truth of our theories beyond any and all reasonable doubt. Popper regarded the claim that we can be absolutely certain of the truth of our theories as frightfully arrogant, but he also thought that it had led many philosophers to throw out the baby with the bathwater. He regarded the relativist's claim that there is no absolute truth as entirely mistaken, and relativism itself as one of the greatest maladies of our time. But he also thought that the 'relativists' who say such things are often confused about what they actually think, and that they are really, and rightfully, rejecting the idea of absolute knowledge instead. For it is difficult, if not impossible, to make sense of their relativism without attributing to them the belief that it is absolutely and objectively true.

Popper said that we do not have an objective criterion of truth, and that we thus cannot know with certainty that our theories are true. But this does not mean that our theories are not genuine statements that are either true or false. It does not mean that truth itself is relative or that absolute truth does not exist. And it does not mean that we cannot search for or succeed in finding it. All it means is that we can never *know for certain* whether or not we have found it. This does not mean that *truth* is *relative*, but only that *we* are *fallible*. But nor does it mean that we have nothing to guide us in our search. For while we do not have an objective criterion of truth, we do have a criterion of falsity. Contradictory statements cannot both be true. And we can thus *test* our theories against their logical consequences in our attempt to discover whether or not they are really true.

Explanation and Prediction

This idea—that we can test our theories against their logical consequences—points to the role that predictions really play in science. Instrumentalism says that the aim of science is prediction. But Popper says that scientific theories aim at giving true causal *explanations* of the world, and that scientists are concerned with *predictions* primarily as a way of testing them.

We can explain an event in the world by deducing a statement that describes it from one or more *universal statements*, together with singular statements, the so-called *initial conditions*, that describe facts in the world pertinent to what caused the event that we wish to explain. We explain what caused a string A to break, for example, by deducing the statement 'The string A broke' from the universal statement 'Any string will break if a weight exceeding its tensile strength is placed upon it' together with the singular statements 'The tensile strength of the string A is 1 *lb*' and 'A 2 *lb* weight was placed upon A'. The universal statement—'If a weight exceeding the tensile strength of a string is placed upon that string, then that string will break'—can be regarded as a causal law of nature.[7] The singular statements—'The tensile strength of A is 1 *lb*' and 'A weight of 2 *lbs* was placed on A'— can be regarded as causes. The deduction itself is a *causal* explanation of why the string broke. It does not simply tell us that the string broke. It tells us why it broke as well.

It is obvious that causal explanation is closely related to prediction. A large part of what distinguishes an explanation from a prediction is whether the statement that we deduce describes an event in the past or an event in the future. If we know that the string A has in fact already broken, then our deduction of the statement that it has broken from the causal law and initial conditions that we have described is an explanation of the fact. But if the string has not yet broke, then our deduction of the statement that it will break from the same causal law and initial conditions is a prediction. It is also obvious that we can always deduce a statement that describes a fact in the world that we want to explain from *some* universal causal statement together with statements describing initial conditions. But it is an entirely different question whether the statements from which we deduce it are true. For it is also obvious that we can deduce such a statement from statements of alleged causal laws and initial conditions that are false. Simply put, the fact that we can give a causal explanation of an event in the world does not mean that our causal explanation is true.

Here, Popper's claim that scientific theories aim at giving true causal explanations is the claim that science is concerned not simply with predicting what will occur, but also with understanding why it will occur. Scientists thus use predictions as a way of *testing* the truth of their explanatory theories. If their predictions are false, then either the causal laws or the initial conditions that they used to deduce them are false. And this means that we have not yet explained, or understood, what is happening in the world.

Consider Einstein's theory of general relativity. General relativity was not the result of new observations. It explained old observations in a new way. But no one had measured the bending of light rays as they pass massive bodies, such as the Sun, and Einstein predicted that they would bend to a greater degree than Newton did. Einstein suggested that this was a way *to test* his theory. He said that he would admit that his theory was false if light rays passing the sun did not bend to the degree that he predicted—or, in other words, if one of the logical consequences of his theory proved false. The question whether or not light would bend to the degree Einstein predicted became interesting, in other words, primarily as a test of his theory. Eddington would never have turned his cameras to the sky to compare the apparent positions of stars photographed during a solar eclipse with their apparent positions photographed six months before and after—let alone organize a major expedition in order to do so—if the difference in these positions did not constitute a test of Einstein's theory. And it is difficult, indeed, to think of another reason why anyone would have been interested in verifying or falsifying these predictions.

I can, perhaps, explain the matter in an entirely different way. If a scientific theory is actually true, then any statement that we derive from it in conjunction with other true statements will also be true. But we may also derive true statements from false statements. And we can also make true predictions without deriving them from any theory at all. Suppose that we had access to an infallible oracle, or a philosopher's stone, or even to God Himself. And suppose that we could make predictions that always turn out to be true simply by asking the oracle or touching the stone or praying to God. We could, in this way, satisfy our desire for true predictions. But we would not satisfy our desire for scientific knowledge. Asking the oracle or touching the stone or praying to God may tell us what will happen in each and every case. But it will not help us to understand why these things will happen. And while there can be little doubt that we would all like to be able to predict the future, there can also be little doubt that scientists would like to understand the world.

Pragmatism, Coherence, and Consensus

The idea that a definition of 'truth' must include a criterion of truth has led many philosophers to say that truth is not correspondence to the facts, but something else. Here, the most popular ideas are that the 'truth' of a theory means its utility, or its logical coherence, or the fact that it is accepted by most people, or by most of the experts in a field. These ideas might, respectively, be called the 'pragmatist', 'coherence', and 'consensus' theories of truth. Each of these theories would replace the idea that truth is a correspondence between a statement and the facts—something for which we admittedly have no criterion—with a criterion for determining whether or not a statement is true. But each of them would, if taken seriously, also have disastrous consequences. For they would mean that a liar would be speaking truthfully if only his lies were useful, or consistent with other things he had said, or successful in fooling most people, or the experts. It is, moreover, also easy to see that none of these ideas captures what we mean when we say that a theory is true. For consider the questions 'I know that this theory is useful, but is it really true?', 'I know that this theory is logically consistent, but is it really true?', and 'I know that this theory is generally accepted and that all the experts accept it as well, but is it really true?' Each of these questions makes perfect sense—and each of them, I might add, plays an important role in motivating scientific inquiry. But each of them would involve a contradiction in terms according to the pragmatist, coherence, and consensus theories of truth. Now consider the question 'I know that this theory corresponds to the facts, but is it really true?' This question actually seems more like a joke. And the fact that it seems like a joke, I submit, indicates that we really understand 'truth' to mean the correspondence of a statement with the facts, regardless of the fact that we do not have a criterion for determining it. Indeed, the only reason I know for suggesting that 'truth' does not mean correspondence with the facts is that we do not have an objective criterion to determine whether or not a theory corresponds to the facts. Some philosophers, insofar as this is concerned, say that Tarski did not really define 'truth' as correspondence, since his theory does not include a criterion of truth, and since pragmatist, coherence, and consensus theorists all agree that 'Snow is white' is true if and only if snow is white. But T-sentences are *supposed* to be tautologies, and Tarski himself said that he was trying to define 'truth' as a correspondence between a statement and the facts. The primary virtue of his definition is that it enables us to see that we can speak meaningfully about the truth of a theory even if we do not have a criterion for determining it.

Truth and Information Content

The idea that truth is the regulative ideal of science can also be easily misunderstood, even if we distinguish between a definition of 'truth' and a criterion for determining the truth. For scientists are not in search of truth *per se*. They want to find *interesting* truth, and *informative* truth, and truth that can play some role in *solving their problems*. Now some people think that truth itself is an illusion, or that it is impossible to find. But Popper thought that exactly fifty per cent of all possible statements are true. For the negation of a statement is itself a statement, and exactly one of the two must be true. But he also thought that truth is not always interesting, or informative—and that there are plenty of truths that solve no problems at all. Tautologies, for example, are one and all true. But they are not always very informative. We can be confident that it will either rain or not rain tomorrow morning. But this will not tell us whether or not to carry an umbrella. Or consider the statement '2 + 2 = 4'. You may or may not regard it as interesting or informative, though it will no doubt help you to solve a problem or two. But if '2 + 2 = 4' is true, then it follows that '2 + 2 = 5' is false— and that '2 + 2 = 6' is false, and that '2 + 2 = 7' is false, and so on. But if these statements are false, then the statements '"2 + 2 + = 5" is false' and '"2 + 2 = 6" is false' and '""2 + 2 = 7" is false' are one and all true. And it is easy to see that we can, in this way, generate an infinite number of true statements that are of no interest to science at all, or to anyone else for that matter.

Popper used to joke that omniscience, for this reason, is not only impossible for humans, but undesirable as well.

Not all truth is interesting and informative. But Popper thought that a statement's information content varies *inversely* with its probability. Tautologies are almost certainly true,[8] but seldom very informative. Now consider the empirical statement 'Microsoft will close on 1 May 2001 somewhere between twenty-five and one hundred, twenty-five dollars'. This, as things have turned out, is actually a true statement. But it is not very informative or very useful for an investor. 'Microsoft will close on 1 May 2001 at seventy dollars and seventeen cents', which is also true, is far more informative. But it is, *quite aside from the fact that it is true*, also more likely to be false. It is more likely to be false because it takes a greater risk by saying more. Popper thought that we can, in general, say that the more information a statement conveys, the less likely it is to be true; and the more likely it is to be true, the less it really tells us about the world.

Indeed, we might even regard a *false* explanatory theory that could accurately predict the closing prices of shares within, say, a five dollar range as more informative and more interesting than a true theory that can predict their closing prices only within a one hundred dollar range. We might, ironic as it may sound, even say that some *false* theories are closer to the truth than some true ones.

Verisimilitude

Considerations like these led Popper to try to define the idea of 'verisimilitude', or what it means for one false theory to be closer to the truth than another, in terms of the truth and falsity contents of a theory. The truth content of a theory is the class of true logical consequences of that theory, and the falsity content of a theory is the class of false logical consequences of that theory. Popper said that a *false* theory *A* has less verisimilitude than a *false* theory *B* if and only if the truth content of *A* is less than the truth content of *B* and the falsity content of *B* is less than or equal to the falsity content of *A*, or the truth content of *A* is less than or equal to the truth content of *B* and the falsity content of *B* is less than the falsity content of *A*. He thought that a *false* theory *B* could be said to be closer to the truth than a *false* theory *A* if either of these conditions were satisfied.

Popper's definition of 'verisimilitude', however, does not work. One of his students showed that any two *false* theories have exactly the same number of true and false consequences. Popper recognized and accepted this criticism of his definition. But the idea that some false statements are closer to the truth than others still seems very intuitive. And while Popper's attempt to define 'verisimilitude' in terms of the truth and falsity contents of a theory does not work, it may well be possible to define the term in some other way. The definition of 'verisimilitude' is still an outstanding problem in the philosophy of science as this book goes to press. And if you are able to give a logically consistent definition of the term, then you will have made an important contribution to the field.

Endnotes

---

[1] Karl Popper, *The Open Society and Its Enemies*, Routledge & Kegan Paul, 1945. Reprinted by Routledge, London, 1991, vol. II, p. 369.

[2] This was part and parcel of their idea that the meaning of a term is its method of verification.

---

[3] T-sentences may be trivial, but we should not think that they are always true. It is important, on the contrary, to note that a T-sentence may also be false. Thus, the T-sentence '"Grass is red" is true if and only if grass is green' is false because it does not accurately state the conditions under which the statement 'Grass is red' is true. Grass may in fact be green. But if grass is in fact green, then the statement 'Grass is red' is false—since the statement 'Grass is red' is true if and only if grass is red.

[4] Popper, *The Open Society and Its Enemies*, vol. II, p. 371.

[5] See, for example, Karl R. Popper, *Conjectures and Refutations*, Routledge & Kegan Paul, 1963. Reprinted by Routledge, London, 1991, p. 26.

[6] Popper wrote that 'To speak of 'the aim' of scientific activity may perhaps sound a little naïve; for clearly, different scientists have different aims, and science itself (whatever that may mean) has no aims. I admit all this. Yet when we speak of science, we do seem to feel, more or less clearly, that there is something characteristic of scientific activity; and since scientific activity looks pretty much like a rational activity, and since a rational activity must have some aim, the attempt to describe the aim of science may not be entirely futile'. Karl R. Popper, *Realism and the Aim of Science*, Rowman and Littlefield, Totowa, New Jersey, 1983. Reprinted by Routledge, London, 1992, p. 132.

[7] I have here expressed the universal statement 'Any string will break if a weight exceeding its tensile strength is placed upon it' as a conditional statement 'If a weight exceeding the tensile strength of a string is placed upon that string, then that string will break'. The two statements, of course, are equivalent.

[8] I say 'almost certainly true' because the truth of a tautology depends entirely upon the laws of logic—and because logicians have sometimes raised questions about these laws, and these questions have sometimes led to revisions regarding what can and cannot be regarded as tautologous.

6
The Open Universe

Popper believed that the aim of science is to find true causal explanations. He proposed, as a rule of scientific method, that 'we are not to abandon the search for universal laws and for a coherent theoretical system, nor ever give up our attempts to explain causally any kind of event we can describe'.[1] And he underscored the idea by saying that scientific research is, in principle, without end, and that a scientist who one day decides that we have reached a final explanation retires from the game.[2] Popper, however, was also an *indeterminist*. And this has been a source of confusion, since determinism has often been understood as saying that the events in the material world can be explained by universal causal laws—an interpretation that would, as we have just seen, make it part and parcel of his very conception of science. Popper, however, thought that this idea of determinism is the real source of confusion. He wrote that:

> *Indeterminism*—or more precisely, physical indeterminism—is merely the doctrine that not all events in the physical world are predetermined with absolute precision, in all their infinitesimal details. Apart from this, it is compatible with practically any degree of regularity you like, and it does not, therefore, entail the view that there are 'events without causes'; simply because the terms 'event' and 'cause' are vague enough to make the doctrine that every event has a cause compatible with physical indeterminism. While physical determinism demands complete and infinitely precise physical predetermination and the absence of any exception whatever, physical indeterminism asserts no more than that determinism is false, and that there are at least some exceptions, here or there, to precise predetermination.[3]

In this chapter I will explain Popper's arguments against determinism, his arguments for indeterminism, and his idea that ours is a world of objective propensities.

Determinism: Religion, Science, and Metaphysics

Popper wrote that:

> The intuitive idea of determinism may be summed up by saying that the world is like a motion-picture film: the picture or still which is just being projected is *the present*. Those parts of the film which have already been shown constitute *the past*. And those which have not yet been shown constitute *the future*.
>
> In the film, the future co-exists with the past; and the future is fixed, in exactly the same sense as the past. Though the spectator may not know the future, every future event, without exception, might in principle be known with certainty, exactly like the past, since it exists in the same sense in which the past exists. In fact, the future will be known to the producer of the film—to the Creator of the world.[4]

This idea, which seems to capture Einstein's notion of determinism,[5] has its origins in religious belief, as Popper's reference to 'the Creator of the world' suggests. The Creator, we are told, is both all-powerful and all-knowing. This means that God is powerful enough to completely determine the course of history and infallibly knows the future in advance. Of course, the fact that God is powerful enough to determine the course of history does not mean that the course of history is actually predetermined. But if God already knows the future, then the future—including all of our future actions—must somehow already be fixed. For how else would God be able to know the future in advance?

Popper thought that the idea of religious determinism gave rise to the idea of scientific determinism when naturalists replaced the idea of God and God's law with the idea of nature and the laws of nature. But scientific determinism is a more sophisticated doctrine. It says that the structure of the world is such that *any event can be deduced, with any desired degree of precision, if only we have a sufficiently precise description of past events, together with all of the laws of nature.*[6] This, of course, does not mean that scientists can actually deduce even a single event, let alone all events, to *any* degree of precision they desire. But it does mean that they can 'in principle' do so. And this means that scientific determinism would

61

be false if there were even one event that could not be deduced in this way.

Scientific determinism is thus a stronger position than what Popper called 'metaphysical' determinism. Metaphysical determinism says that *every* event is determined—just like religious and scientific determinism. So each of these theories is false if there is just one event that is not determined. But metaphysical determinism does not assert that these events are known to anyone or that they can be accurately predicted, let alone to any degree of precision that we like. This means that religious and scientific determinism must be false, and indeterminism true, if metaphysical determinism is false. But it also means that metaphysical determinism may be true even if scientific and religious determinism are false.

Metaphysical determinism and indeterminism, however, are both empirically untestable and, hence, irrefutable. So are religious determinism and scientific determinism.[7] But the fact that they are metaphysical theories does not mean that we cannot rationally evaluate or criticize them. For we can argue that determinism does not solve any of the problems that it was designed to solve, or that it doesn't solve them any better than indeterminism, and that it has merely shifted the problem in some other direction instead. We can also argue that the solution that it proposes is neither simple nor fruitful. And we can argue that it contradicts other metaphysical theories that are needed to solve other problems.[8] Popper, insofar as this is concerned, believed in free will. But he thought that it was useless as an argument against determinism. For he recognized that 'a man may well believe that he is acting deliberately, and of his own free choice, when in fact he is acting under the influence of suggestion, or of compulsion, or of drugs'.[9] He thought that the arguments in favor of *scientific* determinism are actually the strongest arguments in favor of metaphysical determinism. But he also thought that there is no good reason to think that scientific determinism is true, and that there are several good reasons to think that it is false.

Of Clouds and Clocks

Physics, up until the formulation of the quantum theory around 1927, conceived of the cosmos as a giant mechanical clockwork. Laplace said that we could, if given the true laws of nature and a complete description of the state of the universe—the position, mass, velocity, and direction of each of its particles at any one instant of time—deduce the state of the universe at any other instant of time.

This is scientific determinism. It says that clouds are in principle just as predictable as clocks and that the only reason that we are unable to accurately predict the motion of clouds is that we do not yet know as much about them as we do about clocks. If scientific determinism is true, then our inability to predict an event reflects our own ignorance, and not any indeterminism in the cosmos. This idea is also supposed to explain our inability to predict the actions of human beings. For the actions of human beings are also events in the world. And if scientific determinism were true, then we would, if given the true laws of nature and a complete description of the universe at any given time, be able to predict and retrodict the actions of human beings as well. So if we cannot predict the actions of human beings, it is only because we do not yet know enough about them. And if we are never able to predict the actions of human beings, it is only because we never will.

Scientific determinism, stated thus simply, is just as unfalsifiable as other forms of determinism. For we can always explain away the failure of our predictions as due to our lack of sufficiently precise information. But while many people think that metaphysical determinism contradicts our experience of free will, many others think that scientific determinism is supported by classical physics.

Popper thought that scientific determinism became a serious conviction amongst scientists when Kepler and Newton made it possible to predict the motions of the planets, or 'vagabonds', as precisely as those of the fixed stars. Kepler's laws of planetary motion and Newton's dynamics are deterministic theories, and many scientists, as a result of their success, concluded that science must be determinist too. Popper thought that the success of these theories is actually the strongest argument in favor of scientific determinism. But he also argued that it is limited to a specific area of physical theory. Newtonian mechanics does not entail determinism, because we do not yet have any reason to think that all physical events are mechanical. 'Only after a successful deduction from Newton's mechanics of a satisfactory theory of electricity, of magnetism, and of optics, could the question arise whether or not the truth of Newton's mechanics may be used as an argument for 'scientific' determinism.'[10] And he pointed out, contrary to determinist hopes, that it is only by the use of artificial experimental isolation that we can predict physical events; that the solar system is an exceptional case of natural, as opposed to artificial, isolation; and that we are very far from being able to predict the precise results of a *concrete* physical situation, such as a thunderstorm, or a fire.[11] Popper thus argued that the extrapolation of our ability to make precise predictions about the motions of the planets to an ability to make precise predictions in other areas of science is at best an unpaid promissory note—and that there are simply too many other areas in science—behavior, physiology, and psychology are three good examples—in which we have little if any ability to make precise predictions at all.

So the fact that a theory is deterministic does not mean that the world it describes is deterministic too. But Popper also argued that we cannot, for logical reasons, predict the growth of human knowledge, as we would have to be able to do if scientific determinism were true; and that we cannot make predictions with *any degree of precision desired* for the simple reason that no measurement can be infinitely precise.[12]

Indeterminism

Thus far we have considered some of Popper's arguments against scientific determinism. But Popper also offered arguments in favor of indeterminism, and he attacked metaphysical determinism itself when he found they did not move Einstein away from his belief in a block-universe. He argued that 'an important reason for accepting indeterminism, at least tentatively, is that the burden of proof rests upon the shoulders of the determinist'.[13] And he cited the following 'common sense' reasons for thinking that this is so:

(1) Unsophisticated common sense favors the view that there are both clocks *and* clouds, that some events are more predictable than others, and that determination and predictability are matters of degree;

(2) There is a prima facie case to think that organisms are less determined and predictable than some simpler systems, and that the higher organisms are less determined and predictable than the lower ones;

(3) If determinism were true, then it should in principle be possible to predict artistic creations and scientific discoveries by studying an artist's or scientist's brain; and

(4) Indeterminism is a weaker assertion than scientific determinism, since scientific determinism asserts that *all* events are in principle predictable and indeterminism asserts only that there exists *at least one* event that is not.[14]

Popper thus argued that there is nothing in our experience to suggest that determinism is true. Einstein was willing to admit the point, but did not see its force until Popper reminded him that he had himself used an analogous argument against the introduction of action at a distance. Popper then argued that the future would be redundant, and indeed superfluous, if metaphysical determinism were true; and that this redundancy is difficult to reconcile with Einstein's idea that the universe is metaphysically simple. Finally, though perhaps most important, Popper argued that even if metaphysical determinism were true and we were only experiencing successive frames of an unchanging movie film, our own conscious experience of these successive frames would at least constitute a change in Einstein's block-universe.

None of these arguments can be regarded as decisive refutations of determinism, or as decisive proofs of indeterminism. They are designed, on the contrary, to undermine the idea that determinism is an essential part of the scientific outlook, and somehow entailed by the success of physics. They work by forcing us to recognize that determinism is still an unpaid promissory note, that it is not necessary for science in any obvious way, and that it is unable to explain what we might otherwise regard as our common sense human experience.

A World of Propensities

The Laplacean idea that we can deduce the precise state of the universe at any instant in time, if given the laws of nature and a description of the state of the universe at any instant in time, held sway in physics until 1927, when Werner Heisenberg introduced his famous 'uncertainty principle', or 'principle of indeterminism'. The uncertainty principle says, for example, that it is impossible to measure both the position and the momentum of a particle with unlimited precision. For the more accurately we measure its position, the less accurately we can measure its momentum. And the more accurately we measure its momentum, the less accurately we can measure its position. The quantum theory thus introduced the idea that probability is an essential component of the physical description of the cosmos. It said that we can, at best, deduce only the *probability* that a particle will be in a given state at a given time. The principle of indeterminism is a cornerstone of quantum physics. But it is entirely compatible with metaphysical determinism. And it is ironic, insofar as this is concerned, that neither Einstein nor Popper were entirely convinced by it. Popper did not appeal to the principle in his arguments against scientific determinism. But it indirectly figures in his argument for indeterminism. For many quantum physicists, including Einstein, regard probabilities as a measure of our own human ignorance. They say that there are facts about the universe that we do not know, and that we are forced to make probabilistic predictions as a result. Popper, on the contrary, believed that the world is actually undetermined. He said that the universe is open and that our probability statements do not reflect our ignorance, but the objective propensities of the world to behave in one way as opposed to another. In this section, I will try to explain what his propensity interpretation of probability is supposed to mean.

Popper's propensity theory of probability is a metaphysical theory that is designed to answer the question 'What are we measuring when we measure the probability of an event?'

Now the 'classical theory of probabilities' measures the probability of an event as the number of favorable events divided by the number of possible events. If we consider the toss of a fair coin, then we will say that the probability of its landing heads is one-half, or .5. For there are only two possibilities—the coin will either land heads or tails—and only one of these, its landing heads, is a favorable result. Or if we consider the toss of a fair die, then we will say that the probability of its landing with its face showing an even number of dots less than six is two-sixths, or .333—since there are only six possibilities, and only two of these, 2 and 4, are even numbers less than six. In each case, we calculate probability as the ratio of positive to possible events, without experimenting with the coins or dice themselves.

There are, however, *biased* coins and *loaded* dice. If you place a piece of lead in a wooden die near the face that shows the number six, then (everything else being equal) the face that shows the number six will show up less frequently than it would with an unloaded die. There will still be six possible outcomes of a toss. But these possible outcomes will not be equally weighted. The die, on the contrary, is loaded, and this means that there will be a greater probability that some faces will turn up than others. Coins, of course, may be biased in much the same way. And if a coin is biased, then the probability that it will land heads will be either greater or less than .5.

This idea, that the universe may be 'loaded', is the basic idea behind Popper's claim that we live in a world of propensities. The cosmos is not a giant mechanical clockwork. But nor is it entirely random. Some events are more likely to occur than others. And the measure of their probability is not a measure of our ignorance, but a measure of their objective propensity to occur.

Thus far we have explained the propensity of an event in terms of a loaded die. This may leave the impression that the propensity of a die to turn up six is a property of the die itself. Popper thought that this would be a mistake. The die, whether loaded or not, has no greater propensity to show one face as opposed to another unless we toss it. Its propensity to show an even number less than six is a property of a *situation*. Thus the propensity of an unbiased coin to land heads may change if we toss it onto a bed of sand, or a table with slots, where it may actually land on end. Its propensity to land on end will be greater, everything else being equal, if there are more slots on the table than if there is only one.

Propensities may thus be regarded as invariant aspects of a physical situation:

> Just as we explain the tendency or propensity of a magnetic needle to turn (from any initial position it may have assumed) towards the north by (a) its inner structure, (b) the invisible field of forces carried with it by our planet, and (c) friction, etc.—in short, by the invariant aspects of the physical *situation*; so we explain the tendency or propensity of a sequence of throws with a die to produce (from any starting sequence) stable statistical frequencies by (a) the inner structure of the die, (b) the invisible field of forces carried with it by our planet, and (c) friction, etc.—in short, by the invariant aspects of the physical *situation*: the field of propensities that influence every single throw.[15]

Propensities, thus understood, are not so much mathematical probabilities, as a generalization and extension of the idea of a physical force, in which the objective physical situation determines propensities rather than forces. Thus:

> The propensity 1 is the special case of a classical force in action: a cause when it produces an effect. If a propensity is less than 1, then this can be envisaged as the existence of competing forces pulling in various opposed directions but not yet producing or controlling a real process. And whenever the possibilities are discrete rather than continuous, these forces pull towards distinct possibilities, where no compromise possibility may exist. And zero propensities are, simply, no propensities at all, just as the number zero means 'no number'.[16]

Propensities, like forces, are 'the result of (or dependent upon) certain *relations* between other physical entities'.[17] And they are, 'just like forces, or other abstract or 'occult' physical entities, introduced in order to explain the known by the unknown'.[18]

Earlier I said that Popper rejected the idea that probability statements are a measure of our own ignorance about the world. This 'subjectivist' interpretation of probability is part and parcel of determinism. If all events are predetermined, then we could predict what will happen with precision, as opposed to probability, if only we had enough knowledge. Propensities, however, are also compatible with determinism, and with the idea that probability is a measure of our own ignorance. For one might say that once all the relevant factors are known, every event will have a propensity of either 0 or 1.

But once we allow for the possibility that the world is not determined, we can also interpret probability statements as referring to real objective propensities in the world. And we can understand the propensity of an event as resulting from the competing forces in a single objective situation that may influence, but not always determine, its outcome.

Indeterminism Is Not Enough

Earlier I said that Popper believed in free will, but did not regard it as a very good argument against determinism. But once we allow for the possibility that the world is not determined, the problem of free will, and of human freedom in general, takes on a greater significance. For determinism simply cannot explain our common sense experience of making real choices with real consequences in the real world. And simple indeterminism, which asserts merely that not all future events are predetermined, is not enough either. For neither of these theories can even begin to explain our apparent freedom to create works of art, or scientific theories, or to reason and argue about what to do. The idea that the events in the world are either predetermined or occur entirely by chance belies the simple but undeniable fact that we at least feel that our decisions and choices play some role in determining our actions, and that our actions play some role in determining the course of events. It also belies the fact—which some philosophers have, ironically enough, appealed to in order to explain the belief in determinism—that we often find our freedom frightening, and accordingly spend a great deal of time, energy, and anxiety in trying to decide how to act.

In chapters 3 and 4 I explained Popper's theory of the three worlds and his idea that we use our World 3 objective knowledge as a plastic control system for maneuvering our way through the world. That explanation presupposed that we do in fact have free will, and that the choices and decisions that we make can directly affect our chances for survival. In the next three chapters, we will explore the consequences that this idea has for Popper's social philosophy—and, in particular, for his vision of an open society.

Endnotes

---

[1] Karl R. Popper, *The Logic of Scientific Discovery*, Hutchinson, London, 1959. Reprinted by Routledge, London, 1992, p. 61.

[2] See Popper, *The Logic of Scientific Discovery*, p. 53.

[3] Karl R. Popper, *Objective Knowledge*, revised edition, Oxford University Press, New York, 1979, p. 220.

[4] Karl R. Popper, *The Open Universe*, Hutchinson, London, 1982. Reprinted by Routledge, 1991, p. 5.

[5] Einstein, in a private conversation with Popper in 1950, accepted Popper's claim that he believed in a four-dimensional unchanging 'block-universe' in which the future is contained in the past in a way analogous to a motion-picture film. Popper believed that Einstein's determinism was, in fact, of a religious or metaphysical kind. See Popper, *The Open Universe*, pp. 89-92. See also, Karl Popper, *Unended Quest*, Routledge, London, 1992, pp. 129-31.

[6] See Popper, *The Open Universe*, p. 2. I have replaced Popper's term 'predicted' with 'deduced' in this passage in order to make it clear that scientific determinism demands that we must be able to retrodict as well as to predict.

[7] Scientific determinism is not itself a scientific theory. Popper calls it 'scientific', because its proponents claim that it is part of the scientific outlook and entailed by the success of science.

[8] Popper, in fact, used just these kinds of arguments when he tried to convince Einstein to give up his determinism. For a discussion of how we can rationally criticize metaphysical theories, see Karl R. Popper, *Conjectures and Refutations*, Routledge & Kegan Paul, 1963. Reprinted by Routledge, London, 1991, pp. 198-200.

[9] Popper, *The Open Universe*, p. 1.

[10] Popper, *The Open Universe*, p. 38.

[11] See Karl Popper, *The Poverty of Historicism*, Routledge & Kegan Paul, 1957. Reprinted by Routledge, 1991, p. 139.

[12] See Popper, *Objective Knowledge*, p. 220.

[13] Popper, *The Open Universe*, p. 27.

[14] See Popper, *The Open Universe*, pp. 27-8.

[15] Karl R. Popper, *A World of Propensities*, Thoemmes, Bristol, 1990, p. 12.

[16] Popper, *A World of Propensities*, p. 13.

[17] Popper, *The Open Universe*, p. 105.

[18] Popper, *The Open Universe*, p. 105.

7

The Poverty of Historicism

Scientific inquiry is problem solving, and our knowledge grows as we propose theories to explain what we do not understand, and then criticize them in an attempt to eliminate their errors. Our understanding of ourselves and of the world we live in, like life itself, is constantly changing. And Popper thought that we have deeply ambivalent attitudes toward it. We welcome change because it makes it possible to build a better world. But we are terrorized by change because it will eventually lead to our own destruction. Change and the idea of change pose a problem for us. And much of our social and political thought is an attempt to solve it. Popper coined the term 'historicism' to describe a cluster of ancient but ultimately impoverished ideas that many social and political philosophers have tacitly accepted in an attempt to acknowledge the fact of change while simultaneously trying to bring its most frightening aspects under control. He thought that these ideas constitute a dangerous philosophical doublethink in which an initial recognition of change leads to a denial of its ultimate reality. Popper first discussed these ideas in *The Poverty of Historicism*,[1] which attributes their appeal to widespread misunderstandings amongst social scientists regarding the proper methods of empirical science. But he later argued in *The Open Society and Its Enemies* that historicism led such great philosophers as Plato, Hegel, and Marx to deny the possibility of democratic reform, and to support authoritarian social theories and totalitarian political regimes. I cannot do justice to Popper's critique of Plato, Hegel, and Marx in this short book. But in this chapter, I will explain what he meant by 'historicism' and why he regarded it as a misunderstanding of the proper methods of empirical science. I will then explain his distinction between 'utopian' and 'piecemeal' social engineering in Chapter 8, and his vision of open society in Chapter 9.

Historicism

Popper regarded historicism as a determinist superstition that comes in many different forms. It is 'the view that the story of mankind has a plot, and that if we can succeed in unravelling this plot, we shall hold the key to the future'.[2] In theistic versions of historicism, the plot of history is written by a god—or gods—that may intervene in human events. But there are also naturalistic, spiritualistic, and economistic versions in which the laws of historical development are characterized as laws of nature, or laws of spiritual development, or laws of economic progress. Each of these versions is typically accompanied by a tribalism, or racism, or collectivism that emphasizes the importance of a particular group—such as the chosen people, or the Aryan race, or the proletariat—and understands the importance of individuals, and indeed of historical development itself, entirely in terms of that group. And they typically foresee an ending that lies only in the distant future:

> For although it may describe this end with some degree of definiteness, we have to go a long way before we reach it. And the way is not only long, but winding, leading up and down, right and left. Accordingly, it will be possible to bring every conceivable historical event well within the scheme of the interpretation. No conceivable experience can refute it. But to those who believe in it, it gives certainty regarding the ultimate outcome of human history.[3]

Historicism, in each of its various forms, expresses 'one of the oldest dreams of mankind—the dream of prophecy, the idea that we can know what the future has in store for us, and that we can profit from such knowledge by adjusting our policy to it'.[4] And it is, in our own time, often taken for granted as part of the methodology of the social sciences. The historicist method assumes that the primary aim of science is to predict the future, and that the goal of inquiry in the social sciences is to discover the laws that govern historical change. It says that a *scientific* approach to solving our social and political problems must be based upon 'laws of development' that determine the course of human history, and that the task of the social sciences is 'to lay bare the *law of evolution of society* in order to foretell its future'.[5] Indeed, the fundamental idea of historicism is that social scientists should, with sufficient knowledge, be able to predict social events with the same precision as astronomers can predict eclipses. Popper, however, argued that historicism seriously misconstrues the aim of science, the nature of scientific laws, and the role that prediction plays in scientific inquiry.

Popper said that the aim of science is not to predict the future but to explain the causal relationships between events; that science cannot predict what will happen *per se*, but at best what will happen under certain circumstances; and that scientists use predictions to test whether or not their theories about those relationships are true. He said that the basic mistake of historicism is that '*Its 'laws of development' turn out to be absolute trends*' that are supposed to 'carry us irresistibly in a certain direction into the future'.[6] Historicists use these absolute trends as a basis for making unconditional historical *prophecies*, as opposed to conditional scientific *predictions*. And they then say that their prophecies are both rational and unavoidable, since they are scientifically determined. Thus, Karl Marx wrote that:

> When a society has discovered the natural law that determines its own movement, even then it can neither overleap the natural phases of its evolution, nor shuffle them out of the world by a stroke of the pen. But this much it can do: it can shorten and lessen the birth-pangs.[7]

In Chapter 5 I explained why Popper thinks that the goal of science is explanation and how empirical predictions serve as tools for testing their truth. And in Chapter 6 I explained his rejection of scientific determinism. But I have yet to explain the distinction that he drew between scientific prediction and historical prophecy. And in order to do that, I will first have to explain the distinction that he drew between scientific laws and historical trends.

Laws and Trends

We can best approach the distinction between scientific laws and historical trends by asking whether there can be a *law* of evolution. Popper wrote that the answer to this question must be 'No', and that the search for such a law could never be part of a scientific inquiry. 'My reasons', he said, 'are very simple':

> The evolution of life on earth, or of human society, is a unique historical process. Such a process, we may assume, proceeds in accordance with all kinds of causal laws, for example, the laws of mechanics, of chemistry, of heredity and segregation, of natural selection, etc. Its description, however, is not a law, but only a singular historical statement.[8]

But scientific laws are *universal* statements that describe regularities in nature. Newton's laws of motion, for example, describe regularities in the movements of physical bodies. But they do not assert that such bodies, or anything else for that matter, actually exist—let alone move. Now Popper thought that 'every natural law can be expressed by asserting that *such and such a thing cannot happen*'.[9] The law of conservation of energy says that 'You cannot build a perpetual motion machine'. The law of entropy says that 'You cannot build a machine that is a hundred per cent efficient'.[10] And Newton's laws say that it is impossible for bodies to move in certain ways. Historical trends, on the other hand, are *tendencies*, as opposed to *regularities*. We describe them with *singular* statements, as opposed to *universal* laws. We may say, for example, that the population of a certain state tripled every thirty years during the 1800's, or that the divorce rates in a certain country have increased since the 1960's, or that a certain stock doubled its value every year during the 1990's. These statements describe unique historical processes. But they cannot tell us that these trends are part of a regular or necessary historical process. And they cannot tell us that they will continue. Trends may be either conditional or unconditional. We may, for example, say that the population in a particular state will continue to grow *if* there is no war, or that it will *simply* continue to grow. And we may do so regardless of whether we have any theory to explain its growth. Scientific laws and historical trends are thus entirely different things. And Popper thought that the confusion of trends with laws is what gave rise to the historicist idea that there are laws of social evolution.

Prediction and Prophecy

Earlier I said that Newton's laws do not assert that physical bodies actually exist. We cannot, for this reason, use them to predict the actual position of a planet without appealing to so-called 'initial conditions', i.e., statements that describe its position, mass, velocity, and direction at a given point in time. Scientific *laws* thus state *unconditional* universal generalizations—by which I mean universal generalizations whose truth does not depend upon the changing conditions in the world. But scientific *predictions*, on the other hand, *are* conditional. They depend both upon scientific laws and upon the initial conditions, or causes, of the events that we wish to predict. Science may predict that the water in a kettle will boil *if* it reaches a certain temperature. And it may even predict that it will *actually* boil. But it is obvious that we may also predict that the water will boil without any theoretical explanation in terms of scientific laws and initial conditions at all.

Now Popper thought that there *are* laws in the social sciences, and he offered the following examples from sociology:

'You cannot introduce agricultural tariffs and at the same time reduce the cost of living.'—'You cannot, in an industrial society, organize consumers' pressure groups as effectively as you can organize certain producers' pressure groups.'—'You cannot have a centrally planned society with a price system that fulfills the main functions of competitive prices.'—'You cannot have full employment without inflation.'[11]

But statements that describe unique historical processes are not laws. And we cannot derive predictions from them. Such statements may describe the existence of trends, and the assumption of trends may be a useful statistical device. But they cannot tell us that these trends are part of a regular—let alone necessary—historical process. And they cannot tell us that they will continue.

I am now in a position to explain Popper's distinction between scientific predictions and historical prophecies. Prophecies, of course, are predictions. They purport to tell us what will occur in the future. And predictions, if true, tell us something about the course of history. But the predictions that are typically made by historicist social scientists are not *scientific*, since they are made on the basis of historical trends and not on the basis of scientific laws. Popper's critique of historicism can thus be expressed in two theses:

The first is that the historicist does not, as a matter of fact, derive his historical prophecies from conditional scientific predictions. The second (from which the first follows) is that he cannot possibly do so because long-term prophecies can be derived from scientific conditional predictions only if they apply to systems which can be described as well-isolated, stationary, and recurrent. These systems are very rare in nature; and modern society is surely not one of them.[12]

Historical prophecies may be 'based upon experience'. And they may even turn out to be true. But the historicist's claim that his predictions *must be true because they are based upon scientific laws* is a misunderstanding of the nature of scientific laws and scientific prediction. So those who wish to underwrite the authority of unconditional historical prophecies by appealing to the authority of science will have to look elsewhere for support.

The Oedipus Effect

Our solar system is a fairly isolated, stationary, and repetitive system. This allows us to make very precise long-term predictions about eclipses. It allows us to do so, in part, because of its regularity, which we can describe in universal scientific laws. But its relative isolation is also important, since it insulates the initial conditions, or causes, from outside influences. If God were to suddenly make the Earth stand still in its orbit, then our astronomical predictions regarding eclipses would be thrown into disarray. Now Popper, as we have already seen, did not deny that there are scientific laws in the social sciences. But he also thought that societies are not isolated systems, that the initial conditions that we might use to make predictions in the social sciences are subject to the influence of human action, and that the very publication of such a prediction may itself be enough to affect the course of events that it seeks to predict. This is what he called 'the Oedipus effect':

> The idea that a prediction may have influence upon the predicted event is a very old. Oedipus, in the legend, killed his father whom he had never seen before; and this was the direct result of the prophecy which had caused his father to abandon him. This is why I suggest the name '*Oedipus effect*' for the influence of the prediction upon the predicted event (or, more generally, for the influence of an item of information upon the situation to which the information refers), whether this influence tends to bring about the predicted effect, or whether it tends to prevent it.[13]

We do not help to bring about an eclipse when we predict that an eclipse will occur. But a prediction that the economy will 'move' into recession may very well effect whether or not the economy 'moves' into recession. It is easy to see how such a prediction can be self-fulfilling. Employers prepare for the predicted recession by laying-off employees, investors by selling stocks, and consumers by cutting down on purchases. And these 'preparations' may, in the end, bring about a recession that otherwise would not have occurred. A more interesting example is when we bring about a predicted event by trying to avoid it. This was the case in the Oedipus myth. It is not at all clear that Oedipus would have killed his father or married his mother had he grown up knowing who they were. Myths, of course, are myths. But a political regime may attempt to avoid a predicted revolution by cracking down on suspected revolutionaries. And its attempt may backfire if the crackdown leads more people to join the revolutionary cause.

Predictions like these can effect the course of events for the simple reason that human beings are able to understand and act in response to them. This is clearly the case with the predictions that we make in the social sciences. But if the Moon were able to understand a prediction and act in response to it, then the prediction of a solar eclipse might become self-fulfilling or self-defeating too. And even if we could predict what the Moon would do, it is not at all clear that we would be able to predict the effects of its action. The fact of the matter, in any event, is that we know full well that our actions often have unintended and undesired consequences that we cannot always foresee.

Popper did not believe that there is anything like a scientific law of evolution, either in biology or in history. But he did believe that there are scientific laws in the social sciences. I have already cited a few of his examples from sociology. Here are a few more that he offered from the study of power politics:

> 'You cannot introduce a political reform without causing some repercussions which are undesirable from the point of view of the ends aimed at'....—'You cannot introduce a political reform without strengthening the opposing forces, to a degree roughly in ratio to the scope of the reform.'... —'You cannot make a revolution without causing a reaction.'... —'You cannot give a man power over other men without tempting him to misuse it—a temptation which roughly increases with the amount of power wielded, and which very few are capable of resisting.'[14]

Each of these examples points out the unintended consequences that our attempts at political reform may entail, and they each point out that we can neither foresee nor control all of the consequences of our own actions. This was Popper's primary reason for being skeptical about long-term prophecies in the social sciences.

Moral Responsibility

It was not, however, his only reason. Popper developed his philosophy of science partly in reaction to the Marxist social and political philosophy that he had accepted in his youth. The same is true of his critique of historicism. Marxism claimed to be a scientific theory built upon scientific principles. It said that the inevitability of communism was a scientific fact that could be scientifically proven. The Party leaders felt that the scientific inevitability of communism justified their actions and the sacrifices that they encouraged others to make. Popper had first hand experience of this in 1919 when he took part in a demonstration in which several workers were killed. He felt that he was morally responsible for their deaths because he had, as a communist, encouraged them to risk their lives. But he soon found that the Party leaders regarded their deaths as a success for their cause. He began to question whether communism was really inevitable, whether he really knew that its 'proofs' were sound, and whether it was really based upon scientific principles at all. He studied Marx in depth—which, he was embarrassed to admit, he had not done before—and found that too many of its claims did not correspond to what he actually saw. His break with communism made a life-long impression on him. He said that it taught him the dangers of accepting a philosophical theory uncritically, and the ways in which the mind tries to immunize itself against criticism. Years later he would also reject socialism, saying that his experiences with the socialist bureaucracy in Vienna had convinced him that it was a far worse disease than the one it intended to cure. But he never abandoned the humanitarian spirit, and he wrote, toward the end of his life, that he would still regard himself as a socialist if he could only find a way to reconcile it with individual liberty.

Popper argued that the future is open and can be influenced by human decisions. He said that history has no plot—and, indeed, no meaning at all except for the meaning that we decide to give it. He thought that our philosophical and scientific theories have an effect upon our actions and upon the way we live our lives. And he thought that the poverty of historicism is that it encourages us to abdicate our moral responsibility in favor of historical determinism. His social and political philosophy is thus based upon a moral decision. It is the decision to choose reason instead of violence; to fight with words instead of swords; to seek truth instead of death; and to let our false theories die in our place. But Marxism wasn't the only influence. His motto 'I may be wrong and you may be right, and by an effort, we may get closer to the truth' was actually inspired by his confrontation with a young Nazi in 1933—the year that Hitler came to power—who told him, pistol at his hip: 'What, you want to argue? I don't argue: I shoot!'[15] Popper regarded the rational attitude both as an antidote to scientific dogmatism, and as a moral obligation in the face of violence. It is the attitude of critical dialogue, accepted with a full awareness of the difficulty of the task. The search for truth through rational dialogue is a *moral* value, and one that we should pursue as long as we can. But when violence wins over peaceful debate and reason must give in, then we may also have to fight to reestablish this minimal condition for freedom.

Popper, like Marx, believed that science can play an important role in solving our social problems. But he also believed that science cannot prove the inevitability of the future—for the inevitability of the future simply cannot be proven. In his later years, he would often say that the point of scientific inquiry is to kill our theories before they kill us. But in *The Poverty of Historicism* and *The Open Society and Its Enemies*, he advocated the need for a truly scientific social technology that is based upon what he called 'piecemeal social engineering'.

In the next chapter, we will explain exactly what 'piecemeal social engineering' is supposed to mean.

Endnotes

[1] *The Poverty of Historicism* was first published as a series of articles in the journal *Economica* during World War II, and then appeared in book form in 1957. It thus predates Popper's discussion of historicism in *The Open Society and Its Enemies*, which was published in 1945.

[2] Karl Popper, *Conjectures and Refutations*, Routledge & Kegan Paul, 1963. Reprinted by Routledge, London, 1991, p. 338.

[3] Karl Popper, *The Open Society and Its Enemies*, Routledge & Kegan Paul, 1945. Reprinted by Routledge, London, 1991, vol. I, p. 9.

[4] Popper, *Conjectures and Refutations*, p. 338.

[5] Karl Popper, *The Poverty of Historicism*, Routledge & Kegan Paul, 1957. Reprinted by Routledge, 1991, p. 106.

[6] Popper, *The Poverty of Historicism*, p. 128.

[7] Karl Marx, *Capital*, Preface. Quoted in Karl R. Popper, *The Poverty of Historicism*, p. 51.

[8] Popper, *The Poverty of Historicism*, p. 108.

[9] Popper, *The Poverty of Historicism*, p. 61.

[10] See Popper, *The Poverty of Historicism*, p. 61.

[11] Popper, *The Poverty of Historicism*, p. 62.

[12] Popper, *Conjectures and Refutations*, p. 339.

[13] Popper, *The Poverty of Historicism*, p. 13.

[14] Popper, *The Poverty of Historicism*, pp. 62-3.

[15] Karl R. Popper, *The Myth of the Framework*, edited by M.A. Notturno, Routledge, London, 1994, p. xiii.

8

In Search of a Better World

In the last chapter I explained Popper's distinction between scientific predictions and historical prophecies. Historicism mistakes unique historical trends for universal scientific laws. And historicists, in the crudest form of inductive inference, say that these trends will continue, come what may—and then use them as a basis for making unconditional historical prophecies. We have already seen that Popper believed that there are universal laws in the social sciences. But historicism sees prediction as the primary aim of science. And Popper envisioned a methodology that aims at a technological social science. Such a method is anti-historicist, but not anti-historical. It regards history as an important source of information. But it does not aim at making unconditional predictions about the future, and it does not seek to discover the laws of historical evolution. It aims, instead, at solving our social problems. And it studies the general laws of social life in order to find the facts that are important for people who are interested in trying to improve our social institutions.[1] Here, it is important to remember that Popper thought that truly scientific laws can always be expressed in the form of prohibitions. Scientific laws tell us not what *must* happen, but what *cannot* happen. 'You cannot build a machine that is a hundred per cent efficient', and 'You cannot give a man power over other men without tempting him to misuse it.' The technological approach to social science is in search of a better world. It says that the future is open and that our philosophical and scientific theories, together with our moral decisions, can play an active role in bringing about the future that we want. All social reformers practice social technology in this sense. But the approach that Popper proposed tries to impose 'a discipline upon our speculative inclinations'.[2]

It thus searches 'for the various laws which impose limitations upon the construction of social institutions'.[3] Its basis in science is experimentation. And it attempts to learn from experience not by induction, but by paying close attention to our social experiments—and to their failures—in order to see what kinds of institutional reforms are practical and have a realistic chance for success.

These ideas led Popper to distinguish between two different kinds of social engineering.

Piecemeal and Utopian Social Engineering

In both *The Poverty of Historicism* and *The Open Society and Its Enemies,* Popper argued against 'utopian social engineering' and in favor of a 'piecemeal' approach. The distinction between these two ideas is a distinction between two competing conceptions of rationality. The utopian approach says that an action is directed toward an ultimate goal, or aim, or end; and that its rationality depends upon the extent to which an agent determines his means according to his ultimate end— distinguishing his ultimate end from intermediary ends that may serve as means for attaining it—and pursues his ultimate end consciously and consistently. The utopian engineer must first identify his ultimate end. He must next choose the means most appropriate for attaining it, bearing in mind that they are merely means to the end and not the ultimate end itself. And he must then consciously and consistently pursue his ultimate end. Applied to practical political reform, the utopian approach says that we must identify our ideal state or society—the achievement of which is presumably the ultimate goal of our political action—*before* we can do anything to reform our institutions or improve our situation. The piecemeal engineer, by contrast, searches for and fights against the greatest and most urgent evils of society, instead of searching and fighting for its ideal ultimate good. Instead of formulating an idea of his ultimate ideal state, he tries to identify the most pressing social problems in the state that actually exists. And instead of using his vision of the ideal state to determine practical reforms and the means that he must take to bring them about, he tries to design and redesign social institutions that will alleviate actual suffering. The rationality of his action consists not in his consciously and consistently trying to bring about his ideal state, but in an experimental approach that acknowledges his own fallibility and the possibility that his actions may have consequences that are very different from what he intends. He thus proposes tentative solutions to problems, tests them, and tries to eliminate their errors.

Utopian and piecemeal engineering both advocate interventionist approaches to our social problems. And they both argue that social intervention should be based upon science and reason. They are, to that extent, both opposed to the historicism that Popper associated with Marx. But the lesson of the twentieth century, in Popper's view, is that the utopian approach is all too easily undermined by the unintended and unforeseeable consequences of our actions—and that the piecemeal approach can actually work.

Popper regarded the utopian approach as both 'convincing and attractive', but 'dangerous'[4]—and piecemeal engineering as the *only* rational approach to social engineering.[5] He thought that utopian engineering is dangerous because its 'attempt to realize an ideal state, using a blueprint of society as a whole, is one which demands a strong centralized rule of a few, and which therefore is likely to lead to a dictatorship'.[6] He also thought that socialism, *as opposed to Marxism*, is based upon utopian engineering. And it is important, in order to understand his critique of socialism, to understand that *this* was his basic criticism of utopian engineering. Popper used to say that the attempt to build a heaven on earth is more likely to produce a hell. But he did not say that the utopian engineer's ideal state cannot be realized. He argued, on the contrary, that 'this would not be a valid criticism, for many things have been realized which have once been dogmatically declared to be unrealizable'.[7] Nor did he say that the utopian approach is by its very nature impossible. He argued, on the contrary, that it was not *very likely* to succeed, and that the likely consequences of its failure are too dangerous to ignore. Popper was skeptical of proposing sweeping changes, especially in the name of rationality, because he thought that their practical consequences are simply too difficult to calculate. And he argued that 'at present, the sociological knowledge necessary for large-scale engineering is non-existent'.[8] But his basic critique of utopian engineering is that it is too dangerous. Why? Because 'you cannot introduce a political reform without causing some repercussions which are undesirable from the point of view of the ends aimed at'. Because 'you cannot introduce a political reform without strengthening the opposing forces, to a degree roughly in ratio to the scope of the reform'. Because 'You cannot make a revolution without causing a reaction'. And because 'you cannot give a man power over other men without tempting him to misuse it'.[9] He thought, in other words, that the scientific laws of power politics impose limitations upon the scope of the political reforms that are likely to succeed. And he thought that we could see such laws at work in the history of the Soviet Union.

Earlier I said that Popper thought that socialism, *as opposed to Marxism*, is based upon utopian engineering. Many socialists in Russia opposed a piecemeal approach because they thought that real social change requires systemic global reforms. Marx, after all, had argued that capitalism *cannot* be reformed, but can only be destroyed. But Marx thought that this destruction would be the work of history—or, more specifically, the economic laws that fueled his own economistic version of historicism. He thus argued against 'all social engineering, which he denounced as Utopian'.[10] The result is that 'there is hardly a word on the economics of socialism in Marx's work—apart from such useless slogans as 'from each according to his ability, to each according to his needs'.[11] And so when the Communist Party came to power in Russia:

> ...his Russian disciples found themselves at first entirely unprepared for their great tasks in the field of social engineering. As Lenin was quick to realize, Marxism was unable to help in matters of practical economics. 'I do not know of any socialist who has dealt with these problems', said Lenin, after his rise to power; 'there was nothing written about such matters in the Bolshevik textbooks, or in those of the Mensheviks.[12]

Lenin introduced 'military communism' after the October Revolution. This meant that everyone had to work and stand on line to get his food. But it quickly proved to be unsuccessful, and he was forced to revert to the 'New Economic Policy', which was actually a return to a modified market economy. It was only after the Kronstadt Uprising, which was actually a failed attempt at counter-revolution, that the Soviets cracked down on private enterprise. Central planning was introduced instead. And the various 'five-year plans' that followed were based upon the utopian idea that it is possible to rationally plan an economy without a market. A good social scientist would have known that 'you cannot have a centrally planned society with a price system that fulfills the main functions of competitive prices'. But there were too many utopian social engineers in Russia. And their five-year plans, with their unrealistic production schedules and their inability to calculate what was actually needed and what was actually possible, soon proved to be inadequate as well. But instead of trying to correct the mistake, the Soviets tried to hang onto power by offering still more utopian slogans that promised a glorious communist society in the near but always too distant future. And when the rationally planned economy failed to feed its citizens, political repression became a way of life.

The 'Piecemeal'Approach

Utopian engineering impedes our attempt to solve problems by keeping its eyes firmly glued to its ideal, and by not taking into account the ways in which its plans might go wrong. The piecemeal approach, on the other hand, encourages social engineers to acknowledge their fallibility and to search out and eliminate their errors. And it has several other advantages as well:

> In favour of his method, the piecemeal engineer can claim that a systematic fight against suffering and injustice and war is more likely to be supported by the approval and agreement of a great number of people than the fight for the establishment of some ideal. The existence of social evils, that is to say, of social conditions under which many men are suffering, can be comparatively well established. Those who suffer can judge for themselves, and the others can hardly deny that they would not like to change places. It is infinitely more difficult to reason about an ideal society. Social life is so complicated that few men, or none at all, could judge a blueprint for social engineering on the grand scale; whether it be practicable; whether it would result in a real improvement; what kind of suffering it may involve; and what may be the means for its realization. As opposed to this, blueprints for piecemeal engineering are comparatively simple. They are blueprints for single institutions, for health and unemployed insurance, for instance, or arbitration courts, or anti-depression budgeting, or educational reform. If they go wrong, the damage is not very great, and a readjustment not very difficult. They are less risky, and for this very reason less controversial. But if it is easier to reach a reasonable agreement about existing evils and the means of combating them than it is about an ideal good and the means of its realization, then there is also more hope that by using the piecemeal method we may get over the very greatest practical difficulty of all reasonable political reform, namely, the use of reason, instead of passion and violence, in executing the programme. There will be a possibility of reaching a reasonable compromise and therefore of achieving the improvement by democratic methods.[13]

Liberty, Equality, and Fraternity

Popper agreed with many of the aims of socialism. But he preferred 'not to use such terms as 'socialism' or 'capitalism' or anything of the sort for characterizing a serious and responsible political position'. He said that 'the political philosophies of socialism and of liberalism which we have inherited from the 19th century are both just a little too simple and na-ïve'.[14] The French Revolution's ideals of liberty, equality, and fraternity are the ideals that infuse these philosophies. They are worthy ideals. But they are not always consistent, and are more often than not at odds with each other.

We demand liberty, equality, and fraternity. And we appeal to these principles to 'justify' policy decisions at every level. But measures that promote liberty inevitably shortchange equality and fraternity—just as those that promote equality shortchange each of the others. All such measures can, of course, be 'justified'. But 'justifications' based upon the principle of liberty are different from 'justifications' based upon the others. And the differences are not merely theoretical. For we cannot treat all of these values as inviolable at once. And a society that treats equality as inviolable will institute different reforms than one that treats liberty or fraternity in the same way. So while there is no poverty of 'justifications', there is a poverty of justificationism. For 'justifications' that appeal to any one of these principles will be unpersuasive to those who appeal to the others.

Popper thought that the task of social philosophy is a political one. But it is not the task of justifying our political system in terms of utopian principles. It is not the task of justifying our political system at all. It is, on the contrary, the task of piecemeal engineering. Liberty, in an open society, may ultimately take precedence over equality and fraternity. But this does not mean that open society does not value the other ideals highly, or that it treats liberty as a utopian principle. On the contrary, the genius of open society is that it attempts to balance these principles in the same way in which it attempts to balance political power. Piecemeal engineering is not the task of legitimizing our government in theory. It is the unending task of balancing the claims of these competing ideals when we feel that one of them is taking too much precedence over the others. It is the ongoing project of trying to solve our most pressing practical problems by establishing, and reestablishing, an acceptable balance between our ideals—so as to find problems that we are, for the moment, more or less willing to live with.

Popper, insofar as this is concerned, agreed with the socialists that 'business-interests are liable to interfere in a very dangerous way with politics, and that strong means should be adopted' to curb them. He also agreed that 'there is a need for a much greater equalization of incomes', and 'for reasonably bold, but *critical* experimentation in the political and economical sphere'. And he said that there is no reason 'why such experiments should stop short of experimenting with 'socialisation of means of production''. But he thought that such experiments are unlikely to work unless 'the considerable and serious dangers' raised by them are frankly faced, and means are adopted to avert them—and unless 'the mystical and naive belief is given up that socialisation is a kind of cure-all'. He argued, on the contrary, that 'there *could be* worse differences of income' under socialism; that 'there could be, accordingly, worse exploitation', since 'exploitation is misuse of economic power, and socialisation means accumulation of economic power'; that 'there could be very easily more undue interference of the economically powerful people in politics'; and that 'there could be a greater amount of control of *thought*'. 'It all depends', he wrote, 'on how one goes about these things'. But he immediately added that socialists do not generally understand these dangers, and 'therefore go about these things in a way which invites disaster'.[15]

Popper also had a soft spot for Marx. He wrote that:

> One cannot do justice to Marx without recognizing his sincerity. His open-mindedness, his sense of facts, his distrust of verbiage, and especially of moralizing verbiage, made him one of the world's most influential fighters against hypocrisy and pharisaism. He had a burning desire to help the oppressed, and was fully conscious of the need for proving himself in deeds, and not only in words. His main talents being theoretical, he devoted immense labour to forging what he believed to be scientific weapons for the fight to improve the lot of the vast majority of men. His sincerity in his search for truth and his intellectual honesty distinguish him, I believe, from many of his followers.[16]

But he thought that Marx was mistaken about science and historical determinism—and about capitalism as well.

There can be little doubt that Marx was aiming at freedom. But there is no doubt at all that he missed his goal. Marx criticized capitalism for the exploitation of its workers. But he and Lenin thought that freedom would depend upon centralization, and upon a 'dictatorship of the proletariat'. It is easy enough to see a problem in the idea that freedom depends upon dictatorship. Trotsky, we are told, predicted it early on. He said that 'these methods lead, as we shall yet see, to this: the party organization is substituted for the party, the Central Committee is substituted for the party organization, and finally the 'dictator' is substituted for the Central Committee'. But many Marxists apparently believed that a dictatorship would be acceptable so long as it put an end to exploitation. And so it is easy today to forget that Marxists thought of themselves as fighting for freedom.

'Scientific' Socialism

Popper thought that historical determinism is false and that the socialist's idea of science is nothing but a 'naïve, vulgar-Darwinist evolutionism'. He said that it is the 'aesthetic-Utopianist-Messianist element in socialism which is its main danger, and which drives it so easily into a totalitarian direction'.[17] But he thought that Marx's biggest mistake was his idea that capitalism could not change. This idea, predicated upon his historicism and upon his belief in the 'essential nature' of capitalism, led Marx's followers to deny that meaningful change could ever occur through piecemeal reforms. They thus 'justified' their ideological rejection of any and all proposals to reform capitalism from within. They insisted that 'capitalism cannot be reformed, but can only be destroyed' and that 'if one wishes to have a better society it must be destroyed'. They predicted that 'the workers' lot will grow worse and worse; and that is why it is necessary to destroy capitalism'.[18] But they did not quite show that any of these statements are true.

Popper, as a youth, believed in the truth of these Marxist doctrines. But he soon came to describe them as a trap. And the fact of the matter is that capitalism in the West did change. Or, to put it more accurately, the fact of the matter is that people in the West changed it. They did so by thinking about their problems and about ways to improve their own situations. They did so by bargaining for better working conditions and by introducing laws restricting certain practices. These negotiations were at times accompanied by the threat of violence and at times by violence itself. But even when violence did occur, it did not culminate in revolution, or in the destruction of capitalism, as Marx had predicted. The fact that we were able to make these changes in our social institutions was no doubt due to the pressure that some people felt in the face of growing support for an economic system that would deprive them of even greater economic freedom—that is, economic power; that is, money—than the changes upon which they finally agreed. But it was also due, to an even larger extent, to the fact that most of the people who were involved in making them valued a society that provides a rational and non-violent process for change. It was, in the end, due to the fact that they wanted to maintain a free society and realized that doing so would require that they value and respect the freedom of others as well as their own.

Earlier I said that the distinction between utopian and piecemeal engineering is a distinction between competing ideas of rationality. It should, by now, be clear that it is also a distinction between competing ideas of science. Popper's idea of rationality and science is the idea of continual piecemeal engineering—it is the idea of rationality as critical discussion and of science as conjecture and refutation—and it is this idea that inspired his critique of 'scientific' socialism. The open society that he envisioned is not a utopian heaven on earth. But it is a society that tries to set free our critical and creative powers. And in the next, and final, chapter I will explain exactly what it involves.

Endnotes

[1] See Karl Popper, *The Poverty of Historicism*, Routledge & Kegan Paul, 1957. Reprinted by Routledge, 1991, p. 46.

[2] Popper, *The Poverty of Historicism*, p. 59.

[3] Popper, *The Poverty of Historicism*, p. 46.

[4] Karl Popper, *The Open Society and Its Enemies*, Routledge & Kegan Paul, 1945. Reprinted by Routledge, London, 1991, vol. I, p. 161.

[5] See Popper, *The Open Society and Its Enemies*, vol. I, p. 157.

[6] Popper, *The Open Society and Its Enemies*, vol. I, p. 159.

[7] Popper, *The Open Society and Its Enemies*, vol. I, p. 161.

[8] Popper, *The Open Society and Its Enemies*, vol. I, p. 162.

[9] Popper, *The Poverty of Historicism*, pp. 62-3.

[10] Popper, *The Open Society and Its Enemies*, vol. II, p. 83.

[11] Popper, *The Open Society and Its Enemies*, vol. II, p. 83.

[12] Popper, *The Open Society and Its Enemies*, vol. II, p. 83.

[13] Popper, *The Open Society and Its Enemies*, vol. II, pp. 158-9.

[14] These two passages are quoted from Popper's 6 January 1947 letter to Rudolf Carnap, in which Popper replied to Carnap's question whether or not he still regarded himself as a socialist. The Karl Popper Archives, Box 282, File 24.

[15] The passages quoted in this paragraph all occur in from Popper's 6 January 1947 letter to Carnap.

[16] Popper, *The Open Society and Its Enemies*, vol. II, p. 82.

[17] Popper to Carnap, 6 January 1947.

[18] Karl Popper, *The Lesson of This Century*, interviewed by Giancarlo Bosetti, Routledge, London, 1992, p. 19.

9

The Open Society and Its Enemies

Open society is often associated with democratic political, judicial and economic institutions—such as majority rule, rule of law, and the market. But Popper himself distinguished open society from the democratic state, and associated it instead with human freedom, fallibilism, and the respect that we should have for the ideas of others. I have already explained how these ideas are connected to his theory of science, and to his critiques of determinism and historicism. But I mention them here because they are also fundamental to his defense of piecemeal engineering—and because it is very easy to misunderstand open society by assuming that it is supposed to be a new utopia. This was not Popper's view. He was in search of a better world dedicated to freedom, reasonableness, and equality. But he thought that utopian thinking is wishful thinking. All of life is problem solving, and our problems will never all be solved. And he warned us that utopian attempts to produce a heaven on earth most often lead to hell.

Popper regarded a *state* as 'a set of institutions, such as a constitution, a civil and criminal law, legislative and executive organs', and a *society* as 'a form of social life and the values which are traditionally cherished in that social life'.[1] He wrote that 'the transition from the closed society to the open takes place when social institutions are first consciously recognized as man-made, and when their conscious alteration is discussed in terms of their suitability for the achievement of human aims or purposes'.[2] But this recognition, and the uncertainty it entails, can be terrifying. And *The Open Society and Its Enemies* is the story of how we have repeatedly tried to escape from the 'strain of civilization' that it causes. It is, more specifically, the story of how some of our leading philosophers have tried to help us escape—either to protect 'the masses', who are not yet ready to deal with their freedom; or to protect their own power and authority—by proposing utopian engineering projects, based upon historicism, that would replace individualism, fallibilism, and critical thinking with solidarity, 'group-think', and submission to the collective. And it is the story of how these attempts have often led to authoritarian and totalitarian states that would curtail our freedom of thought and action.

A closed society may value freedom, reasonableness, and equality. But it values security more. Popper characterized it as a 'magical or tribal or collectivist' society in which each individual knows his place. He said that individuals in an open society are confronted with personal decisions, and that there is nothing quite like this in a closed society. Closed societies are structured around beliefs and institutions that are supposed to be certain and immutable, and their proponents are willing to impose these beliefs and institutions—by force if necessary—and to uphold them against all dissent. Popper, however, thought that only those beliefs that are freely adopted and sincerely held have any real human value, and that the attempt to force people to accept things against their conscience is both futile and corrupting. An open society thus allows different philosophical, religious, and scientific beliefs to coexist and compete with each other. And it encourages its members to use their freedom and their critical powers to try to improve their own situations.[3]

There can be little doubt that people in democratic states are called upon to make decisions in elections, courts of law, and the marketplace. But I will, in what follows, explain Popper's vision of open society by distinguishing it from the institutions with which it is often confused. In order to do this, I will need to introduce his distinction between nature and convention. And I will also need to explain how the 'strain of civilization' tempts us to renounce our freedom, our individuality, and the responsibility for our decisions, and to seek comfort in a closed society instead.

Nature and Convention

Popper wrote that:

It is one of the characteristics of the magical attitude of a primitive tribal or 'closed' society that it lives in a charmed circle of unchanging taboos, of laws and customs which are felt to be as inevitable as the rising of the sun, or the cycle of the seasons, or similar obvious regularities of nature. And it is only after this magical 'closed society' has actually broken down that a theoretical understanding of the difference between 'nature' and 'society' can develop.[4]

Open society, he said, begins with a clear awareness of the distinction between *natural laws* on the one hand, and *normative laws* on the other—and with an equally clear awareness of the fact that the normative laws of human societies, unlike laws of nature, are products of human decisions. Closed societies tend to blur this distinction, if they are aware of it at all. The upshot is that closed societies regard their social taboos, norms, and customs as laws of nature—if not laws of God—that are written in stone. Open societies, by contrast, regard them as human conventions that are written by humans, and can be rewritten by humans, on the shifting sands of human experience.

The distinction between natural laws and normative laws is part and parcel of the distinction between facts and values. It is implicit in the idea that we cannot derive an 'is' from an 'ought' or an 'ought' from an 'is'. Natural laws *describe* unvarying regularities in nature, and the statements that purport to express them are either true (if the regularity holds) or false (if it does not). Laws of nature are unalterable and beyond human control. And there are no exceptions to them. Normative laws, by contrast, *prescribe* behavior. Popper thought that our normative laws might be regarded as good or bad, right or wrong, acceptable or unacceptable. But he argued that they do not describe facts and should not be regarded as true or false. It may, of course, be a fact that certain societies abide by certain normative laws. But these normative laws themselves are human conventions. They are made by human beings. And they can be broken by human beings. To say that a law of nature has been broken is to say that it is not really a law of nature. But there is no sense at all in instituting a normative law unless it can be broken.

Popper characterized the transition from a closed to an open society as a transition from a '*naïve monism*' that does not distinguish between natural and normative laws to a '*critical dualism*' that does. Closed societies may be dominated by a *naïve naturalism* that says that natural and normative regularities are beyond any change whatsoever, or by a *naïve conventionalism* that says that they are entirely dependent upon the will of gods or god-like men. But in either case, the transition to open society occurs as soon as we recognize that we are free to choose the normative laws under which we live.

This recognition, however, leads to 'the strain of civilization'.

The Strain of Civilization

The recognition that we are free to choose the normative laws under which we live is—or should be—accompanied by the recognition that we alone are responsible for the normative laws that we choose. This recognition, when coupled with an awareness of our own human fallibility and of the disastrous consequences that change can wreck, may tempt us to renounce our freedom and try to return to the relatively carefree closed society.

This is the strain of civilization. It results from the fact that open society deprives us of clear and unquestioned moral certainties, as well as a clear and unquestioned place in it. The members of an open society compete with each other in an attempt to improve their social positions. This forces them to make decisions regarding what they should do and how they should act. And they may soon find that freedom does not make them happy.

The anxiety of making decisions in an uncertain world is just one aspect of the strain of civilization. Competition and the struggle for social status is another. And a third, no doubt, is the fact that an open society deprives us of the comfort and security that one feels from being an accepted member of a real or concrete social group. Indeed, Popper wrote that:

> As a consequence of its loss of organic character, an open society may become, by degrees, what I should like to term an 'abstract society'. It may, to a considerable extent, lose the character of a concrete or real group of men, or of a system of such real groups. This point which has been rarely understood may be explained by way of an exaggeration. We could conceive of a society in which men practically never meet face to face—in which all business is conducted by individuals in isolation who communicate by typed letters or by telegrams, and who go about in closed motor-cars. (Artificial insemination would allow even propagation without a personal element.) Such a fictitious society might be called a 'completely abstract or depersonalized society'.[5]

The strain of civilization, he wrote, 'is the strain created by the effort which life in an open and partially abstract society continually demands from us—by the endeavour to be rational, to forgo at least some of our emotional social needs, to look after ourselves, and to accept our responsibilities'.[6]

But this is not all. For:

> It is part of the strain that we are becoming more and more pain-
> fully aware of the gross imperfections in our life, of personal as
> well as of institutional imperfection; of avoiding suffering, of
> waste and of unnecessary ugliness; and at the same time of the fact
> that it is not impossible for us to do something about all this, but
> that such improvements would be just as hard to achieve as they
> are important. This awareness increases the strain of personal re-
> sponsibility, of carrying the cross of being human.[7]

Popper thought that the strain of personal responsibility that is caused
by this awareness may in the end lead us to yearn for the lost paradise
of a closed society, where we are not called upon to make such difficult
decisions, and where we feel unthreatened and insulated from change.
He argued that it almost inevitably leads to reactionary attempts to return
to the comfort and security of the group. And he tried to show how it led
Plato, Hegel, and Marx to historicism and to utopian engineering projects
in an attempt to quell the terrors of change. He described their proposals to
reform society as reactionary attempts to reclaim a lost certainty and security. He was willing to acknowledge that Marx, and perhaps even Plato,
had the best of intentions. But he argued that their philosophies have, despite their good intentions, given comfort to authoritarian and totalitarian
states—and that the utopian attempt to reclaim the lost security and certainty of the closed society is a philosophical double-think that is
doomed to fail:

> We can never return to the alleged innocence and beauty of the
> closed society. Our dream of heaven cannot be realized on earth.
> Once we begin to rely upon our reason, and to use our powers of
> criticism, once we feel the call of personal responsibilities, and
> with it, the responsibility of helping to advance knowledge, we
> cannot return to a state of implicit submission to tribal magic. For
> those who have eaten of the tree of knowledge, paradise is lost.
> The more we try to return to the heroic age of tribalism, the more
> surely do we arrive at the Inquisition, at the Secret Police, and at a
> romanticized gangsterism. Beginning with the suppression of rea-
> son and truth, we must end with the most brutal and violent de-
> struction of all that is human. *There is no return to a harmonious*
> *state of nature. If we turn back, then we must go the whole way--*
> *we must return to the beasts.*

It is an issue which we must face squarely, hard though it may be for us to do so. If we dream of a return to our childhood, if we are tempted to rely on others and so be happy, if we shrink from the task of carrying our cross, the cross of humaneness, of reason, of responsibility, if we lose courage and flinch from the strain, then we must try to fortify ourselves with a clear understanding of the simple decision before us. We can return to the beasts. But if we wish to remain human, then there is only one way, the way into the open society. We must go on into the unknown, the uncertain and insecure, using what reason we may have to plan as well as we can for both security *and* freedom.[8]

Popper thought that open society is a 'cross' and a 'strain'; that it is the 'unknown', the 'uncertain', and the 'insecure'; and that it is something before which we may 'lose courage' and 'flinch'. He said that we suffer from the shock of its birth. But there is no going back to the womb. For we have tasted our freedom and reason, as well as our own fallibility. Open society may or may not be original sin. But it certainly is not a utopia.[9]

Open Society and the Democratic State

Earlier we saw that Popper associated a state with its institutions, and a society with its values. He thought that an open society, more specifically, values 'freedom, tolerance, justice, the citizen's free pursuit of knowledge, his right to disseminate knowledge, his free choice of values and beliefs, and his pursuit of happiness';[10] and that a democratic state is characterized by institutions that enable its citizens to dismiss their government, and to work for peaceful change.[11] Popper admitted that this distinction is not very sharp. But he regarded it as important. He thought that freedom is an end in itself, and that a democratic state is the form of government most likely to foster and protect it. He thus proposed and defended democracy against the authoritarian and totalitarian governments that are typical in closed societies. And he wrote that 'without democratic control, there can be no earthly reason why any government should not use its political and economic power for purposes very different from the protection of the freedom of its citizens'.[12] But he also cautioned that institutions are never foolproof and may always be used to serve ends opposed to those for which they were designed. And he thought that it is easy to conflate democracy with open society, to treat it as if it were an end in itself, and to lose sight of the values that it is supposed to protect.

Popper said that it is important to understand democracy instead of idealizing it—and that it is especially important to understand that democracy will work fairly well in a society that values freedom and tolerance, but not in a society that does not understand these values.[13] Here, the first thing to understand about democracy is that it is not open society itself, but a set of institutions that can, at best, help to preserve an open society. The second thing to understand is that democracy may help to *preserve* freedom, but can never *create* freedom if the citizens in a society do not value it. And the third, but perhaps most important, thing to understand is that democracy also poses a serious threat to open society.

Democracy poses a threat to open society because we have to invest a good deal of power in a state in order for it to be effective—and because whenever there is power, there is always the danger of its abuse. 'The truth is that all forms of government are imperfect, and even dangerous, and that democracy is no exception'. But *'the state should exist for the sake of the human individual—for the sake of its free citizens and their free social life—that is, for the sake of the free society—and not the other way round.'* And Popper argued that a citizen must thus combine the duty of loyalty that he owes to his state with 'a certain degree of vigilance and even a certain degree of distrust of the state and its officers: it is his duty to watch and see that the state does not overstep the limits of its legitimate functions'.[14] These ideas led him to value democratic institutions for different reasons than many of his contemporaries.

Majority Rule, Rule of Law, and the Market

Most people who value democracy value majority rule. They think that democracy is rule by 'the people', and that rule by the people is better than rule by a king or a dictator. Popper, however, thought that majority rule is largely a myth—and that to focus upon '*Who* should rule?' is to focus upon the wrong problem. He said that democracy has never been—and, indeed, neither can nor should be—rule by the people.[15] And he thought that there was even a danger in teaching that democracy is rule by the people—since the people will feel cheated when they discover that it is not. 'Democracies', he said, 'are not popular sovereignties, but, above all, institutions equipped to defend themselves from dictatorship. They do not permit dictatorial rule, an accumulation of power, but seek to limit the power of the state'.[16] The role of 'the people', in a democracy, is not to rule or govern. It is, on the contrary, to judge how well their elected officials are doing it.

Popper thought that the most important political problem is not who should rule, but how to get rid of leaders who are incompetent or corrupt. He thought that the primary virtue of democracy is that it has mechanisms that enable a society to change its rulers without revolution or violence. He said that governments are either democracies or tyrannies, and that the difference between the two is that democracies, but not tyrannies, have established institutions—such as elections[17]—for dismissing their leaders without bloodshed.

It is important to understand that this is a problem that is implicit in the very nature of government. For government implies power. And power tends to corrupt. And if this is true, then our leaders will tend to be corrupted by it—no matter how good they may once have been. Popper thought that it is a utopian fantasy to think that we can solve this problem by getting 'the best' leaders. For even if we could agree upon who is 'the best', the best are human and will tend to be corrupted like all the rest. It is, indeed, ironic that the futility of this approach can already be seen in Plato's *Republic*. For Plato is very clear that the philosopher king is chosen for his devotion to truth and his inability to tolerate falsehoods in any form—and that the very first thing that the philosopher king must do to insure 'justice' in the Republic is to tell the 'noble lie'.[18]

Similar remarks can be made regarding rule of law and the market. They are not tantamount to freedom itself, but are institutions that can help to preserve it. Popper thus thought that the laws of a state should 'maximize the freedom of each within the limits imposed by the freedom of others'.[19] He liked to quote Oliver Wendell Holmes' maxim that the freedom to move one's fist is restricted by its proximity to someone else's nose.[20] And he insisted that the state should limit the freedom of its citizens as equally as possible, and not beyond what is necessary for achieving an equal limitation of freedom.[21] But while some proponents of open society have associated freedom with an unregulated market or with a *permanent* framework of laws in which an individual can choose a course of action with a full awareness of its legal ramifications, Popper associated it instead with the ability of the members of a society to work for peaceful change.

The laws of a democratic state, insofar as this is concerned, are in this respect just like its leaders. They are normative laws and not laws of nature. They are written by humans and can be rewritten by humans. And we recognize, as members of an open society, that we are free to dismiss them and to write new laws in their place when they no longer serve our purposes. This, indeed, is what piecemeal engineering is all about.

Popper thought that the market is probably more efficient than a planned economy. But he argued that 'it is wrong to base the rejection of tyranny on economic arguments'.[22] He believed that freedom is the most important thing in the political field. But he was especially critical of the nineteenth century apologists of unrestrained capitalism who appealed to the principle of freedom to resist labor legislation and to defend the coercion of workers that Marx described as 'exploitation'. And he described their argument that it is our right to enter into any contract that we consider favorable to our interests—and their slogan 'equal and free competition for all'—as both cynical and hypocritical.[23] He thought that freedom could not be saved without increasing economic equality.[24] But he also thought that it was possible to increase economic equality through piecemeal experiments in regulating the market. And he was, in any event, even more worried about the power that communism would have to give to the state in order for centralized planning to succeed:

> Even if it were true that a centrally planned state economy is superior to that of the free market, I should oppose the centrally planned economy. I should oppose it because of the likelihood that it would increase the power of the state to the point of tyranny. It is not the inefficiency of communism against which we should fight, but its inhumanity and its inherent hostility to liberty. We should not sell our freedom for a mess of pottage, or for the promise that we shall obtain the highest possible productivity and efficiency—not even if we could be sure that we can purchase efficiency at the price of liberty.[25]

Unended Quest

Popper wrote that 'an open society (that is, a society based on the idea of not merely tolerating dissenting opinions but respecting them) and a democracy (that is, a form of government devoted to the protection of an open society) cannot flourish if science becomes the exclusive possession of a closed set of specialists'.[26] He told me, on one occasion, that his philosophy is summed up in his motto 'I may be wrong and you may be right, and by an effort, we may get closer to the truth'—and, on another occasion, that it is summed up in his schema, $P_1 \rightarrow TT \rightarrow EE \rightarrow P_2$. The first represents his fallibilism, his respect for other people, and his idea that truth is our regulative ideal. The second emphasizes that science and society progress—like life itself—from problem to problem.

He also told me that he agreed with many of the humanitarian goals of socialism, and that he would still regard himself as a socialist were it not for the power problem.[27]

Popper entitled his intellectual autobiography *Unended Quest*— and its German translation *Ausgangspunkte*.[28] These titles capture his idea that we are—in science, society, and life itself—always making a new start at an old project that has no natural or predetermined end. Popper agreed with Marx that the task of philosophy is to change the world and not merely to describe it. But he did not think that there are laws of history or laws of economics that govern change, or that philosophy will have completed its task by articulating them. Life continually presents us with new problems. We try to solve them by proposing new scientific theories and social institutions. But the theories that we propose may or may not be true, and the social institutions that we propose may or may not serve our ends. So we continually test them, and criticize them, in an effort to improve them. We try, in this way, to kill our false theories and our ineffective institutions before they kill us. But we do so, in an open society, with the conscious recognition that we are largely responsible for our own decisions.

Endnotes

[1] Karl R. Popper, 'The Open Society and the Democratic State', in The Karl Popper Archives, Box 6, File 6.

[2] Karl Popper, *The Open Society and Its Enemies*, Routledge & Kegan Paul, 1945. Reprinted by Routledge, London, 1991, vol. I, p. 294.

[3] See Popper, *The Open Society and Its Enemies*, vol. I, pp. xiii and 173. There are, of course, no such things as *the* open and *the* closed societies. There are only societies that are open and closed in different ways and to different degrees. We will, nonetheless, speak of *the* open and *the* closed societies as regulative ideals at which actual societies may aim.

[4] Popper, *The Open Society and Its Enemies*, vol. I, p. 57.

[5] Popper, *The Open Society and Its Enemies*, vol. I, p. 174.

[6] Popper, *The Open Society and Its Enemies*, vol. I, p. 176.

[7] Popper, *The Open Society and Its Enemies*, vol. I, pp. 199-200.

[8] Popper, *The Open Society and Its Enemies*, vol. I, pp. 200-201.

[9] Popper, *The Open Society and Its Enemies*, vol. I, p. 201.

[10] Popper, 'The Open Society and the Democratic State'.

[11] See Popper, *The Open Society and Its Enemies*, vol. II, pp. 160-61.

[12] Popper, *The Open Society and Its Enemies*, vol. II, p. 127.

[13] See Popper, 'The Open Society and the Democratic State'.

[14] The passages quoted in this paragraph all occur in Popper, 'The Open Society and the Democratic State'.

[15] See, for example, Popper, *The Lesson of this Century*, interview by Giancarlo Bosetti, Routledge, London, 1997, p. 68.

[16] Popper, *The Lesson of this Century*, p. 70.

[17] Elections are not the only such institutions. Popper said that 'Nothing demonstrated the democratic character of the United States more clearly than the resignation, in effect the removal, of President Nixon' (Popper, *The Lesson of This Century*, p. 71).

[18] Of course, 'justice' in the Republic means staying in one's own place. And the 'noble lie' is that human beings are born of bronze, silver, and gold—and that their heritage is what accounts for their place in society. Popper argued that the philosopher king's defense of 'justice' was thus actually a racially based defense of his own power.

[19] Popper, *The Lesson of this Century*, p. 36.

[20] See, for example, Popper, *The Lesson of this Century*, p. 36.

[21] See Popper, *The Open Society and Its Enemies*, vol. I, p. 110.

[22] Popper, 'The Open Society and the Democratic State'.

[23] See Popper, *The Open Society and Its Enemies*, vol. II, p. 122.

[24] See Popper's 6 January 1947 letter to Carnap. The Karl Popper Archives, Box 282, File 24.

[25] Popper, 'The Open Society and the Democratic State'.

[26] Karl Popper, *The Myth of the Framework*, edited by M.A. Notturno, Routledge, London, 1994, p. 110.

[27] Popper also wrote that he would still be a socialist if socialism could be combined with human freedom. (See Karl Popper, *Unended Quest*, Routledge, London, 1992, p. 36.) But this should not be taken to mean that he regarded himself as a socialist. For he emphasized, on the contrary, that there *is* the power problem, and that he did *not* think socialism could be combined with human freedom.

[28] '*Ausgangspunkte*' means 'starting points'.

Bibliography

Karl Popper's books in the English language include:

The Open Society and Its Enemies
  Volume I: *The Spell of Plato*
  Volume II: *The High Tide of Prophecy: Hegel, Marx, and the Aftermath*
The Poverty of Historicism
The Logic of Scientific Discovery
Conjectures and Refutations: The Growth of Scientific Knowledge
Objective Knowledge: An Evolutionary Approach
Unended Quest: An Intellectual Autobiography
The Self and Its Brain: An Argument for Interactionism
Postscript to the Logic of Scientific Discovery
  Volume I: *Realism and the Aim of Science*
  Volume II: *The Open Universe: An Argument for Indeterminism*
  Volume III: *Quantum Theory and the Schism in Physics*
Popper Selections
A World of Propensities
In Search of a Better World: Lectures and Essays from Thirty Years
The Myth of the Framework
Knowledge and the Body-Mind Problem
The Lesson of This Century
The World of Parmenides
All Life Is Problem Solving